641.5092 ROS

Rossant, Colette

The world in my kitchen :
the adventures of a
(mostly) French woman in
New York

WITHDRAWN

THE
WORLD
IN
MY KITCHEN

THE
WORLD
IN
MY KITCHEN

The Adventures of a
(Mostly) French Woman in America

COLETTE ROSSANT

ATRIA BOOKS
New York London Toronto Singapore

1230 Avenue of the Americas
New York, NY 10020

Library of Congress Cataloging-in-Publication Data
Rossant, Colette.
  The world in my kitchen : the adventures of a (mostly) French woman in America /
Colette Rossant.
    p. cm.
  1. Rossant, Colette. 2. Cooks—France—Biography. 3. Cooks—New York
(State)—Biography. I. Title.
TX649.R67A36 2006
641.5092—dc22
[B]

                                                              2006042908

ISBN-13: 978-0-7434-9028-3
ISBN-10:   0-7434-9028-2

First Atria Books hardcover edition September 2006

10 9 8 7 6 5 4 3 2 1

ATRIA B O O K S is a trademark of Simon & Schuster, Inc.

Manufactured in the United States of America

Cover by James Rossant

Designed by C. Linda Dingler

For information regarding special discounts for bulk purchases, please contact Simon &
Schuster Special Sales at 1-800-456-6798 or business@simonandschuster.com.

To My Children and Grandchildren

1522

When they were wild
When they were not yet human
When they could be anything
I was on the other side with milk to lure them
And their father, too, each name a net in his hand.

—"BIRTH" BY LOUISE ERDRICH

Contents

1. The Move 1

2. Life in New York 35

3. Exploring 67

4. Soho 87

5. Cooking with Colette 111

6. The Travels 141

7. The Journalist 179

8. The Silk Road 201

Acknowledgments 227

THE
WORLD
IN
MY KITCHEN

My wedding to Jimmy in Paris, 1955

I

The Move

>⧁⧀<

We are on our way to Le Havre. The train is going so fast
that the landscape is all but a blur. From time to time, I can see a
farm in the mist surrounded by a sea of green fields. I am excited
but also scared. It is 1955, and we are on our way to New York.
Jimmy and I were married a couple of months ago. Anne, his wid-
owed mother, was at our wedding as was his brother, Murray, but
without his wife. The week before our wedding, Anne and my
mother fought all the time: two jealous women bickering about
dresses, jewelry, food, me, and God knows what else. They were
horrible, like two witches. They nearly ruined my wedding. But as
usual Mira, my stepfather, saved the day. Mira, born in Normandy,
believed that food, that is, very good food, could solve any problem. He took Anne to lunch in a two stars restaurant. She loved it.
Back home, she talked lovingly about eating snails with Swiss Char.

"I had a great lunch! Snails with *Swiss* Char? I had never had that before. I simply *loved* it," she had said smiling happily for the first time in weeks. My mother looked slightly miffed.

"Well, Anne, I'm *so* happy you liked it. Mira *does* know the best restaurants. Maybe tomorrow you and I can try La Coupole?"

"Yes, of course! But only if you let *me* take you out for lunch."

From that day on, my mother and Anne had a truce that lasted until the day of the wedding.

Anne's choice of a dress for the wedding, a pale green tulle dress shocked my conservative mother. "Can you imagine? At her age! Wearing a young ballerina's dress!" my mother had whispered on the telephone to her best friend a few days before the wedding, recounting all the real or imagined problems she had had with my future mother-in-law. My stepfather once again saved the day by taking them both out to dinner at Potin on Avenue Victor Hugo, using the excuse that they should try the food as Potin was catering the wedding reception. "Anne loves sole," he had whispered to me, "they make the best one in Paris." He was right. The two women both chose and devoured the sole meunière. The next few days were calm despite the problems I had with my brother and my grandmother.

My brother, who was doing his military service in Algeria, had refused to come to my wedding on the grounds that Jimmy was an American and therefore not well educated.

"Marry a Frenchman," he had written, "not an American. He does not belong in our family."

I had not gotten along with him since I came back to Paris from Egypt in 1947 because he resented me invading his space.

My French grandmother, who also objected to my marrying Jimmy as he was not the young man of her choice, had refused to attend the wedding and had left the country for the States to visit old friends. I had loved my grandfather. Although he had died just before we came back to Paris, I remembered him quite well as we lived in Paris until I was six and left in 1939 when my father became ill, and my Egyptian grandfather, thinking that the hot Egyptian climate would help him get better, summoned us to Cairo. My brother disliked Cairo, the heat, the noise, and above all, seeing my father ill and helpless. I was too young and did not realize how seriously ill he was. Within a few weeks of our stay in Cairo, my brother who was then ten years old, wanted to leave and go back to Paris. My parents, ill advised, and despite the rumors of an impending war, sent my brother back, alone, to France to live with my French grandparents. I would not see my brother again until I was fifteen.

My father died a year later. Two years after that, my mother, now a thirty-year-old widow, decided that she needed to find herself, to seek a new life and a new husband. A young child, she felt, would hamper her style; therefore, she decided that I would live with my Egyptian grandparents, and for the next five years, I never saw or heard from her.

We were a large extended Jewish Sephardic family. We lived in an enormous house, near the Nile, in the posh neighborhood of Garden City. My grandparents, their two grown daughters, and I lived on the first floor. My grandparent's oldest son, his wife, and five of their children lived on the second floor. On the third and fourth floor lived two of his other children with their wives and children.

The family was large (my grandmother had had nine children), boisterous, and loving. Being the youngest of all the children and also being treated by everyone as an orphan, I was looked after by uncles, aunts, and older cousins. I had the run of the house, but my favorite hiding place was the kitchen. I loved the warmth of the kitchen. It is there that I fell in love with food and Ahmet, the cook who treated me like his own child. By the age of fifteen, my mother reappeared and insisted that I return to Paris to further my education. I was heartbroken to leave my Egyptian family, especially when my mother, once in Paris, left me with her mother, a paragon of rectitude. Mother once again disappeared for another three years.

My French grandmother disliked me intensely for several reasons: one, for having, like my mother, converted to Catholicism; two, for speaking French with an Egyptian accent; and finally, for not being elegant. Furthermore, she felt I was unsettling the close-knit circle consisting of her and my brother (my grandfather had died at the end of the war). I was having quite a miserable time, trying to woo my grandmother and my brother, both of whom ignored me, and trying to lose my Egyptian accent and learning to become a Parisian. I failed to woo them, but eventually lost my Egyptian accent. As for becoming a real Parisian, the task was too tough as I was short, plump, and I had no one to teach me how to dress properly and be elegant.

Jimmy and I had met in 1949, when I was sixteen. Anne had offered Jimmy a trip to Europe after his graduation. She had met my grandparents before the war, and they had remained good friends; she had given him their address in Paris in case he ran out of money, which he did. To a sixteen-year-old teenager, this twenty-year-old, tall, handsome American was a dream come true. We fell in love, and to my mother's dismay, I announced that I wanted to marry him right away. My mother, who for years had not paid attention to me, became suddenly very involved. I cried, got angry, but I could do nothing to change her mind. She kept on repeating the same thing over and over: "Ridiculous! You are too young; you are still in high school; he has to go back to school and choose a profession. No more talk about marriage."

Her mother, for the first time, agreed with her. Then finally, to stop the argument, my mother said that if in five years we still felt the same way, we could get married. Jimmy and I swore that we would wait. He promised to come back for me. We corresponded from time to time, and five years later, as promised, he reappeared in my life. Jimmy was then doing his military service and was stationed in Munich, Germany. To the horror of my family, especially my grandmother, I joined him in Munich where we lived together for a year until we could get married. Jimmy was in the intelligence corps and getting permission to marry a foreigner while in the service took a whole year.

We were finally married on September 8, 1955. The wedding was lovely; the reception at Potin went well even if a former boyfriend, Francis, drunk and angry that I had turned him down, threw a glass of champagne in Jimmy's face. Everyone laughed; the rest of the evening was more peaceful. After the wedding, we went back to Germany. Jimmy had another nine months to serve. He was discharged in Munich, and together we went to live and work in Italy. By the end of 1956, Jimmy felt it was time to return to New York and start a new life there as an architect and also a family.

We went back to Paris to say our good-byes. On our last Sunday, Mira suggested that Jimmy and I go to the Boulevard Raspail market to buy food for lunch and dinner. As we walked through the market, the smells were overwhelming. Jimmy wanted to buy everything. We stopped in front of an asparagus stand. The first asparagus of the season: white fat asparagus with purple tops next to bunches of pale green wild asparagus that looked more like ferns. We bought some of each. Then we stopped at a charcuterie stand and bought some *pâté de campagne*, duck rillette, and *boudin noir* (blood sausages). We bought two pounds of cherries and I ate half of them as we continued our walk. The cheese stand was our next stop. There I bought a chèvre and a piece of Cantal's and

Mira's favorite cheese, a ripe Reblochon. Just before leaving the market, I picked up crusty country bread and a dozen farm fresh eggs. Back at home, I showed Mira our purchases. Jimmy was hovering over us saying he was starving and wanted lunch. Mira and I decided to make asparagus with boiled eggs, one of Mira's specialties. We agreed that we would start with the white asparagus, then serve the boudin with mashed potatoes, and prepare the wild asparagus with mushrooms for dinner. As we peeled the asparagus, Mira handed me a raw one to eat. Crunchy and delicious, tasting like freshly cut grass.

Once cooked, I placed some asparagus on each plate with a boiled egg and clarified butter. I had to explain to Jimmy how to eat them.

"Pour a tablespoon of melted butter in the egg, add salt and pepper, and mix it with a spoon, then dip the asparagus in the egg."

We all laughed when Jimmy picked up his knife and fork to eat the asparagus. In France, I explained to him, you don't cut asparagus; you pick it up with your fingers and eat it, sucking the stalks. The light, creamy taste of the egg yolk enhances the soft, earthy taste of the asparagus. Mira said that sometimes he adds some truffle juice but that he had none that day. For dinner, we steamed the wild asparagus, sautéed the mushrooms, and served the asparagus topped with the mushrooms. Jimmy smiled. "Delicious. I never tasted something so light and fresh. I don't want to leave Paris!" We both looked at him.

"Are you serious?" I asked.

"No. I want to go back. New York is where I belong. But I will miss this sensational food."

The next day we left for New York. We were sailing on *The Liberté*, once a German liner, leftover from the war and now totally refurbished and renamed. Mira had pulled some strings, and we were given a first-class stateroom. Remembering how ill I had been on the passage from Egypt to Marseille on our return to France years before, my mother provided me with pills for sea-sickness. I hoped I would not need them. My mother swore that this new medicine would help. For the last three weeks, she had been very solicitous, even overbearing. I was not used to it. Normally, she would have nothing to do with me. Now she dragged me through stores to shop for a trousseau I insisted I did not need.

"I don't want to go shopping. I don't need anything."

"Yes you do. You cannot go to New York without nice sheets and some tablecloths. You need towels and . . ."

Resistance, I realized was futile. I gave in.

We bought towels, sheets with my initials, pillowcases, and tablecloths. My wedding presents had included fifteen tea table-cloths. "I don't invite friends for tea," I told my mother, who obliged me to keep at least two. The fancy silver went back to the stores; Jimmy hated it. We kept the china and the glasses, a gift from Murray, Jimmy's brother. They had been sent to America. My mother and I bought dresses, a coat, shoes, and handbags. I didn't understand why my mother, who had never bought me anything, thought it was so important that I be well dressed and have sheets with my initials. Who would see my bed? I was sure Jimmy did not care, but I went along with her wishes. At my stepfather's suggestion, she bought enormous wicker baskets to pack everything. Simpler to send, he explained to me. I think that perhaps she was happy to finally get rid of me.

Jimmy urged me to be more patient and kind with my mother.

"I can't. She never took care of me! Why now? I can't erase twenty years of neglect."

But looking at Jimmy's pleading eyes, I said, "Well I will try."

⋙⋘

In the train, rolling fast toward Le Havre, I looked again at Jimmy, who was stirring about to wake up. He smiled and said, "I'm hungry Colette; let's go and have lunch." The restaurant had an elaborate menu. In 1956, food was plentiful, unlike in 1947, when I took a train from Marseille to Paris. Then I was fifteen and excited to be in France, but the war was just over and food was scarce. The menu was very simple. Now there was a prix fixe menu offering a *pâté de campagne* or a frisée salad with walnuts to start and then a choice of lamb shank cooked in cider, a salmon soufflé, a roast beef with truffle potatoes, or a sole meunière; dessert was a cheese tray, ice cream, or an apple and pear tarte. Jimmy chose the *pâté de campagne* and the lamb shank cooked in cider. I took the frisée salad and the sole meunière, my favorite fish. Jimmy explained that in New York there were no real sole, only gray sole. I wondered if the gray sole was what we call in France "limande." I planned to go to a fish market in New York and find out. I looked at Jimmy savoring his *pâté*. A layer of transparent light brown jelly surrounded it. I stole a bite from his plate. The *pâté* had specks of fat, and the herbs, especially the thyme, were too overpowering. I was about to say something, but there was a look of such pleasure on his face that I didn't.

The train slowed down and stopped very near the harbor. The port of Le Havre was large and very busy. There were several ships ready to leave, and ours at the end of the quay was easily the largest one. It was white with blue, red, and white stripes painted on its funnel. We slowly walked the length of the quay. *This is it,* I thought, *once we are on the boat there is no turning around.*

Going up the plank, I looked back at the people milling around. Most of the people boarding the boat seemed young. One teenage French girl on the deck was crying. I wanted to go to her and help her, but Jimmy told me we had to follow the porter to our cabin. Our cabin was one floor below the main deck. In it, there were two beds, a closet, a small bathroom, and two armchairs, and a porthole through which we could see the sea. The ship rocked gently, and already I thought I was going to be sick. I quickly took a pill and hoped that the uneasy feeling I had in the middle of my stomach would soon disappear. Back on the main deck, I looked again for the young girl. I did not see her and looked below at the crowd waving their good-byes. There were no shouts and very little confusion. I thought back to when I had left Egypt for France nine years ago. The crowds were shouting, women were crying, and I had felt lonely and sad to leave my Egyptian family for France and an unknown future. Today was very different. I wasn't scared, just sad. Jimmy's arms were around my waist; he was kissing my neck and whispering words to reassure me. The ship slowly glided out of the harbor. "Let's go to the bar and have a drink to celebrate our new life," he suggested. As I entered the bar, I suddenly knew that I would not make it. I had to be on the deck, or I would be sick. Back upstairs on the deck, I found a chaise lounge, and a young sailor wrapped a blanket around me.

"How do you feel, miss? Would you like a cup of hot broth?"

"Yes, please," I said faintly, thinking I was soon going to be so sick that I would certainly die before reaching New York.

As I drifted into a sort of waking dream, my thoughts turned to New York. *What will it be like living in New York? How will his family greet me? Would I quickly make friends? Jimmy told me that everyone works in America, will I also work? And what kind of work can I do?* As I dozed off to sleep, I felt better. The boat seemed steadier. Maybe I was wrong. *I will be alright, and the crossing will be fine.*

An hour later, I was awakened by the same young sailor bringing me a cup of very hot bouillon and crackers. Jimmy reappeared and insisted we take a walk around the deck. Later, I was back at my chaise until the evening, when once again I tried to go to the dining room. A steaming onion gratinée was placed in front of me. I slowly took a bite. The warm soup with the golden melted cheese and thick slices of transparent onion tasted great and warmed me. I wasn't feeling too bad and finally ate the soup with gusto. While we ate, Jimmy talked about his relatives. His favorite being his aunt Edie, his mother's sister. She had never married. She was an executive with Dunhill, and she lived, Jimmy explained, with another sister, Gina, also unmarried. Gina kept house for them.

"Edie is great; she is fun and very intelligent. You will love her, and she will love you." Naturally, there was also his brother, Murray, with his wife, Naima. They had two young children. I knew Murray. In 1948, he had come to my grandmother's house in Paris. In 1949, he had met Naima and brought her to our house. But I did not remember her well as they had left for the United States a few months after their wedding.

"My mother lives with them in the summer," Jimmy said, as if he could read my thoughts. I had been afraid that we would have to live with her. Jimmy's mother reminded me of my favorite mystery detective, Miss Marple. I thought she looked like her. Her hair was wavy, with curls like tiny sausages at the nape of her neck. She often looked serious and dowdy. I hoped that since we were now going to live in New York, I would get to know her better and we would be friends.

After dinner, I wanted to go back to my chaise lounge, but Jimmy insisted that I try to sleep in the cabin. As I lay in my bed, I tried not to think of the ship's movement. I closed my eyes while saying to Jimmy that I could not stay in the cabin, that I was afraid I would be sick. I woke up the following morning in bed!

For the next five days, life on the ship assumed a routine. I spent a lot of time on my chaise lounge, took long promenades, drank hot bouillon, and only ate once a day. Jimmy talked about the future. He was happy to be going back home. He talked about our living in New York or Boston. He then made drawings of Manhattan, explaining how Manhattan was divided in two, East and West, in a grid, and that all the streets had numbers. It was all very confusing. I remembered reading a book written by two French journalists about their travels in America. I must have been sixteen when I read it. I was fascinated with the authors' tales of New York, the Rocky Mountains, California, and ice-cream sundaes.

"I want to try an ice-cream sundae," I told Jimmy, who looked at me with astonishment.

"But why an ice-cream sundae?"

How could I explain that the vision of a mountain of ice cream topped with whipped cream, chocolate sauce, and a red cherry fascinated me. Could I tell Jimmy that for years America for me was defined by an ice-cream sundae? Never!

On the sixth day the sea got rougher and I refused to go down to the cabin. I slept on my chaise wrapped in blankets. Jimmy woke me up at five. "Get up. We are going to pass the Statue of Liberty. You must see it." We stood next to each other. Jimmy was hugging me as we passed this extraordinary statue wrapped in fog. The scene was eerie. It seemed to me that the Lady was smiling. She was so tall! Much taller than the one on the bridge, the Pont de L'Alma, over the Seine in Paris. And suddenly there was New York. I had not expected the incredible vision of a mass of skyscrapers, shimmering in the early sunlight. I was in awe. Viewed from the ship, New York looked beautiful. As the ship glided slowly down the Hudson lead by a red tugboat, I saw that there must have been a major snowstorm in New York because the roofs of the buildings we were passing were covered with snow. I thought of Paris, which I had left just a few days ago. The parks there were already full of yellow daffodils and tulips under an intense blue sky. So beautiful!

As the ship anchored, I saw people waving on the quay below. I waved back. I recognized Murray and Anne. Jimmy waved also and smiled to me.

"They are down there. Did you see them?"

It took an hour before we could disembark and gather our belongings. Anne embraced me and then Jimmy. She looked sad. Murray stood near her. He was shorter than Jimmy, I thought, with wavy brown hair. He too looked sad. Jimmy asked what was wrong. Anne blurted out that Edie, Jimmy's aunt, had died a week ago. They had not wanted him to know for fear of spoiling his last week in Paris. Jimmy cried, he was crushed by the news. I held his hand trying to comfort him. He blurted out to me, "I wanted her to meet you. I wanted her to see who I married. . . . Oh Colette, this is so terrible." I felt sorry for Jimmy, but I hadn't known Edie, and with the excitement of arriving in New York, I quickly forgot about her.

The car was waiting for us near a highway. Our luggage baskets would arrive later. On the way to Murray's house, no one talked. I looked out of the window and thought that, at the street level, New York was so dirty and ugly. There was so much snow pushed against the edges of the sidewalks. It looked like dirty gray mountains. Where was the beautiful city I had seen from the ship?

We finally arrived at Murray's apartment house on West Seventy-seventh Street. A doorman in uniform took care of our hand luggage. The apartment house faced a very large brick building surrounded by a garden. "That's the Museum of Natural History," Jimmy said. "A great museum; I'll take you there."

Naima stood waiting at the door of the apartment where she embraced Jimmy first, then me. She was a tall, handsome woman in her mid-thirties with jet-black hair tied in a bun at the back of her neck; she was wearing a bold colored, loose dress. I would later learn that these dresses were fashionable and made by a Danish designer called Marimekko. Next to her stood a cute little boy. "This is Maxwell; he is three. Say 'Hi' to Auntie Colette." Maxwell looked at me and smiled but said nothing. "Later you'll meet John; he's eighteen months, and he is sleeping now. Come, I will show you to your room. We gave you our room. Murray and I will sleep in the maid's room."

Immediately we protested, but to no avail. I was too young to understand that this would turn out to be a great mistake; taking their room would later provoke fights and problems. But we were happy to be there, and we settled in their room as we were told. For the next few hours, I explored the apartment. It was as large as my grandmother's in Paris, with four bedrooms lining a somber corridor. The dining room was old fashioned with a large dining table in the center. Later, I joined Naima there as she was preparing lunch. I heard a baby crying. "Why don't you go and pick him up," she said. As I entered his bedroom, John was standing in his crib. Such a lovely baby! I picked him up and kissed him on his neck. In return, I got a gurgling laugh. I knew right away that I was falling in love with him because he looked like Jimmy. I picked him up and took him back to the kitchen. Naima looked flustered, so I asked if I could help. "No thank you. I must feed John and Maxwell; you go back to the living room. Another time maybe." I was too shy to insist, and so I went back to the living room to join Jimmy. Anne was telling him what had happened to Edie.

"She had breast cancer but refused to see a doctor until it was too late."

"What do you mean she refused to see a doctor? Why didn't you drag her there?" There was silence. I realized that Jimmy was angry, Anne upset. I had to do something. How crushing to arrive in a new country and be faced with such horrible news. I was worried about Jimmy. I looked at him, went closer, and squeezed his hand with a smile. We shared a glance and I knew we would be fine.

That night as we sat down to dinner, Naima brought to the table a roast. It was enormous; I had never seen anything like it. Jimmy told me it was a rib roast prepared in our honor. "Very American," he said with a smile.

A thick slice was placed on my plate alongside a very large, unpeeled potato. "Baked potato," Naima explained, "also very American." I looked at Jimmy to see how I was supposed to eat it.

"Split in two; add some butter."

The potato was fluffy, hot, and tasted like the best mashed potato I had ever had. The skin was crisp, and Naima told me I could eat it, too. I discovered that the crackling skin was even more delicious. The slice of beef was bright pink and tender. I took a bite of the brown crackling fat with a piece of meat. I thought that I would have loved to suck on the bone, but no one seemed to do it, so it was with regret that I left it on my plate. To this day, a rib roast is still my favorite meat, but I always suck the bone clean! Next to the meat was a vegetable I never saw before. It looked like a small tree and tasted somewhat like cabbage. I thought it was good, but lacked some garlic or spices. "What is it?" I asked. "Broccoli," Anne explained. "Do you like it?" I didn't really know what to say since I realized that she had prepared it. For my taste, it was too bland. "Strange," I answered, and everyone laughed.

Murray served a very good French wine and told me that in a few years California would produce wines as good as the French. I thought it unlikely at the time, but he was right. Years later, as a food writer, I would go to wine auctions in California and taste wine as good, and sometimes better, than the French.

There was no bread on the table, and I missed it, especially when

Naima brought in the salad. The salad was iceburg lettuce, the same type of salad that the American army wives bought at the PX in Germany, served with some strange dressing that they called "French." However, Naima's dressing was much better. She was, I thought, a very good cook. I looked around the table at the family. I didn't as yet understand the relationship between Naima, Murray, and Anne. There seemed to be tension, but I did not know why. I felt slightly nervous and unsettled, maybe even a bit scared. I looked at Jimmy. He smiled encouragingly, and I felt better. Everyone was looking at me, expecting something. *But what?* I thought I should do something. Picking up my wine glass, I made a toast to the family and said that the meal was great and that I was so pleased to be here.

The next morning I found my mother-in-law in the kitchen preparing breakfast. Maxwell and John were both there. She was making oatmeal. She offered me some, but I could barely eat in the morning and asked for just a cup of coffee and a piece of toast. Jimmy had left to see some friends and get reacquainted with the city. I didn't really know what to do with myself. I did not want to unpack since I hoped to find an apartment of our own soon. I asked Naima if I could help her. She suggested I take John for a walk in the park's playground. Maxwell would be dropped off at a play school. Central Park, I had learned the night before, was the large park near the apartment house. Would I get lost? I was slightly afraid, but thought Naima would explain where the playground was.

While Naima dressed John, I talked to Anne about her plans for the day. "This afternoon, after lunch, I have to visit Gina; she is very sad and upset," she said.

"Can I come with you?"

"No, some other day; she's not ready to meet you."

I left her and wandered again through the apartment. Murray, who was a financial writer for *The New York Times,* had already left for work. John was dressed and ready to be taken outside. Naima drew me a plan of the neighborhood and told me where the playground was. "He can play in the sandbox," she explained. "He likes the swings. Be careful as you cross streets and don't get lost."

We walked across the street to Central Park. I was astonished. The weather had changed, the sky was blue, and the park, as in Paris the previous week, showed signs of spring. There were daffodils on the lawns and buds on the trees. I pointed them out to John, picked a flower, and gave it to him. He tore it apart in two seconds and laughed. He had such a lovely smile, but he never said a word, just laughed.

The playground was surrounded by a cast-iron fence. There were benches all around, and a large sand box in the center, swings on one side, and in one corner a sort of wooden sculpture on which children could climb. So different from a Parisian park where "Défense de marcher sur la pelouse" (Keep off the grass) is the rule. I plopped John in the sandbox and sat and watched him play. I looked around. Women were sitting, talking, and once in a while, one got up and said something to her child. I was bored; I should have brought a book with me. A mother, a tall blonde woman, came and sat next to me.

"Are you new to the playground? Did you just move here?" she asked.

"Yes."

"Is this your son?"

"Yes."

This was a lie. It had flown out of my mouth. Why did I say yes? I felt foolish, but claiming to be John's mother seemed to give me some stature with this woman who started to chat about the weather and the maids in the playground. Pointing to a small, little girl, she said that she was very nasty. I should watch that she did not hit my son. Suddenly I heard a scream; it came from the little girl. John had taken something from her. I jumped up and ran to him. He had a piece of what looked like bread in his hand. The little girl's babysitter arrived, saying in an angry tone of voice, "Your son took Molly's pretzel. Get him his own." She pulled the piece of bread away from John. I picked him up and put him back in the carriage. The blonde woman walked over again and told me that the pretzel man was at the park's entrance. "Children love pretzels. You should get him one."

Naima had given me a couple of dollars, and so I bought a pretzel, cut it in two and gave half to John. As I bit into the slightly warm pretzel, I spit it out immediately. It was disgusting! Chewy, salty, and with a taste of gasoline . . . I pulled it away from John, who started to cry, and threw the pretzel in the garbage can. "Don't cry," I whispered to him. "Colette will buy something good right away." As I looked at Naima's map, I saw that there was a large avenue on the other side of Seventy-seventh Street, and so I walked toward it. I read the sign—Columbus Avenue. Naima had told me that this was where I would find all the shops. I pushed the carriage along the avenue, peering inside the shops. I passed a shoemaker, a butcher, and a dress store. The butcher looked nothing like a French butcher. As I looked at the window display, I recognized nothing, so I continued my walk. Then I saw a bakery where I thought I could get something for John. As we entered the empty store, the woman at the counter asked me what I wanted. I said, "Good morning!" and she looked startled. *Well, maybe here you don't greet anyone as you enter a store.* In France you have to say, "Bonjour messieurs, mesdames . . ." If not, no one will serve you. There were long loafs of sliced bread on the shelves, but no baguettes. There were cakes, sweet pastries, and in a bin, round circles of bread—some with sesame seeds. As I pointed to these, the woman said, "How many bagels? Plain or with sesame seeds?" So these were the famous treats Jimmy had been talking about in Paris. This was a bagel. They looked good, so I asked for "One sesame bagel, please." I gave a piece to John, who stopped crying and sucked on the bread. I took a bite, and I was very surprised. The bagel was chewy, and the crust hard but very tasty, so much better than the pretzel. Happy now, we walked for an hour before heading back to the house.

Back home, Anne was preparing John's lunch. Maxwell would return from school after three, and Naima was out shopping downtown. Once John was asleep in his crib, Anne prepared our lunch and called me in. In front of me was a sandwich. I wasn't sure I knew what it was. White bread, no crust and very soft. The sandwich was stuffed with, my mother-in-law told me, tuna fish salad. It was a sickening beige color. I took a bite, and I nearly choked. It was sweet with bits of what I thought were celery.

"What's in it?"

"Mayonnaise."

I knew two things: It was not really mayonnaise, and I couldn't eat this sandwich. I looked around not knowing what to do. While Anne went back to the kitchen, I quickly wrapped half the sandwich in the paper napkin she had given me and hid it in my pocket. I told Anne I could not eat the remaining half and brought it back to the kitchen. As I sat at the table sipping a cup of weak coffee, I thought of Paris and the ham sandwich in a crisp baguette I would have eaten in a café. I suddenly missed Paris and felt out of place and lonely. I wished Jimmy was there with me to cheer me up, and tell me everything would be all right.

I will never know if Anne knew I had thrown out the sandwich, but she never served me another tuna fish sandwich.

Later that afternoon, Jimmy came back and announced that in

a few weeks there was going to be a large planner's conference at Harvard. We would go together to Cambridge. Lots of architectural and planning firms were going to be there, and he could find a good job. I felt better, and my spirits rose further when he whisked me away for some sightseeing.

Times Square overwhelmed me. I found the space exhilarating, with its lights, its immense advertisements panels, the crowds pushing you around, and the traffic. I stood speechless for a while, looking at the large panels of advertising with moving forms. One was advertising cigarettes, and real smoke was coming out of a woman's mouth. There were so many people, so much noise, and so much color. I loved it and found it astounding. Then we walked over to Fifth Avenue, toward Rockefeller Center. I stood for a while watching people skating in the center of the complex. Suddenly Jimmy whispered in my ear. "What do you want most from New York?"

"An apartment."

"No, what's something you want to eat."

"An ice-cream sundae!"

Hand in hand we walked to a small restaurant near an elegant department store called "Saks Fifth Avenue." The restaurant, Schrafft's, was on the side street. As we were ushered to our table, I looked around. The customers were mostly women sitting at small wooden tables, eating ice cream or drinking tea. There were banquettes against the walls, and the low round soft lights gave the restaurant a sort of genteel look. Jimmy ordered a sundae—the dish I had dreamt of for so many years. A bowl of ice cream was placed in front of me. I looked at it in disbelief. It was a monstrous architectural construction. The ice cream was hidden under a mountain of whipped cream with chocolate sauce dripping artistically, topped with toasted almonds. A bright red cherry gloriously crowned it all. It was exactly like the one I had read about years before. But I took one bite and found the ice cream far too sweet and very creamy. The whipped cream was not like Chantilly, the cherry inedible. The dish was so rich that after two teaspoons I couldn't eat any more. I whispered to Jimmy, "Can you finish it?"

Why did I ever think that an ice-cream sundae would be so marvelous? I don't even like sweets!

We then went by subway to Wall Street. We first stopped in front of City Hall, which looked like a lovely copy of a French chateau. We walked around the park in front of it and then continued to the Woolworth building. Jimmy explained that the building was famous for its intricate façade.

"I love skyscrapers; there is so much poetry in them. You know it was the tallest building in the world at the time. Look up, Colette. Don't you think it is like a giant towering cathedral?"

I looked up and looked at the building with Jimmy-eyes, listening to what he was saying. The building was beautiful! But I did not know if it was as beautiful as a French cathedral, and I said so.

"Colette, look at the terra-cotta skin. Its machine made and celebrates the world of today, but it is able to produce a version of medieval stone of the Gothic architecture, just like the Gothic churches celebrated in their own way, the merchants and the artisans." I wasn't sure I really understood, but I tried to look at New York though his eyes.

Then we walked to Wall Street. The streets in this part of town amazed me; they were so narrow, and the buildings were so tall. I felt like an ant crawling in the street, looking up and barely seeing the sky. Suddenly, what seemed like an army of people came out of every building, pushing and shoving us.

"What is happening?"

"People are going home, Colette. Downtown is filled with offices and at 5:00 P.M. they all go home. In a few minutes, Wall Street will be deserted. Let's wait, and then we can walk around Fulton Street and down to the Battery to look at the Statue of Liberty."

A half an hour later, Wall Street looked like a ghost town, empty and silent. Slowly we walked to the tip of the island and stood together, admiring the Hudson River and the Statue of Liberty in the distance. New York, once again, seemed to me so extraordinarily beautiful.

The next few days went by slowly. I had little to do. I took John for rides in the park and walked around the neighborhood for hours. There were no cafés where I could just sit and look at people passing by. I also felt shy about entering a restaurant alone, not knowing what to order. I explored the shops on Broadway, looked at the clothes and the beauty salons. I noticed women had very strange hairdos; their hair was teased and puffed up. I thought as a young woman of twenty-three, I must have looked very old fashioned with my curls.

Every night, Murray and Jimmy came home late. Jimmy was busy renewing contact with his old friends and job hunting. At night he often told me who he saw and what he did. The search for an apartment did not seem like a priority to him. We had been in his brother's house for three weeks, and I felt tension building up in the family. I felt there was tension between Murray and Naima—we were still staying in their bedroom—and between Murray and Anne, who spent every summer with them. Dinners were difficult. There were many silences. Murray would talk about people he had seen without any explanation of why or for what: "I had lunch with the CEO of . . ." or "As the mayor said to me this morning . . ."

Growing up in Cairo, the conversations my family had were lively and interesting. The family was large, prosperous, boisterous and loving; my grandmother had had nine children. Here it was more like my French grandmother's house. No one talked because there was no love between her and me or between my brother and me. Here it seemed it was the same. Anne resented Naima and seemed not to like her very much. Also, Naima and Murray did not seem, at least in my eyes, to love each other. I started to dread these dinners. I tried to tell Jimmy about it, but he thought I was imagining things.

There was also the problem of the food. Naima was a good cook, but on the nights Anne cooked, I ate nearly nothing. I was not invited to help in the kitchen and was too shy to offer. I spent these awkward dinners dreaming of a tomato salad, a good Camembert, and above all, a French baguette stuffed with ham. I would make my escape at lunch. I had discovered a restaurant that did not have tables, just a counter that made it feel more like a French café. The luncheonette, Chock full o'Nuts, served a cream cheese sandwich on very good walnut bread. I became addicted to it and went there every day, telling Anne not to wait for me for lunch. A few days later, I received a phone call from an old friend of my mother's inviting us to dinner. The night of the dinner, I went looking for a flower shop to bring flowers. I could not find any, and I was worried. Go to dinner to someone's house and bring nothing? Jimmy kept on telling me it was all right.

My mother's friend was a tall, slim American woman with dyed red hair. Mr. and Mrs. Lowenstein lived on Park Avenue in a very grand apartment. They had lived in Paris for a year after the war, where they met my mother. "It was a relief to find someone who spoke English so well," Molly said. "She helped me shop, and we had a great time together." Philip, her husband, a banker, was slightly pompous. He made fun of the French, saying they took long hours for lunch and did not work hard. At the same time, he told me how delightful my accent was. This was something I would hear time and time again. There were many other guests, but I could not distinguish one from the other as everyone was introduced by their first name. I didn't know who was married to whom. The men stood at one end of the large living room and the women at the other. They all drank hard liquor. I was offered whisky but turned it down. I would have loved a glass of wine but ended up drinking orange juice. The women talked about shopping, babies, and baby-sitters while I tried to listen to the men's conversation. Their conversations were about politics and the stock market. I would have liked to join them but decided it was best if I stayed with the women. I had nothing to contribute to the women's conversations, as I had no children and no home of my own.

Dinner was served from a buffet by a black maid in uniform. We didn't sit at the dinner table but on chairs and couches. I was not used to it and was afraid to spill my food. The whole evening was painful and boring. As we took our leave, I thanked Molly for the lovely dinner. "We must see you again soon," she said, as I thought that I would have to find friends of my own very soon.

A week later we left for Boston. I was so happy to leave the house and be alone with Jimmy. The city delighted me. I loved the row of town houses around the Green; the scale of the buildings was a relief after Manhattan's skyscrapers and mammoth apartment buildings. On our first night, Jimmy took me to his favorite restaurant—a small fish place where we ate broiled flounder and where I had my first taste of clam chowder. The light creamy broth, filled with chopped clams and cubed potatoes, had a wonderful aroma of the sea and fresh thyme. Oysters followed, thick fatty oysters so different from the French ones but still wonderful. They slid down my throat in one gulp. The next day we went to Cambridge for the conference on planning. I liked Cambridge with its small streets, funky boutiques, and cafés with students sipping espresso and discussing their classes, books, or politics. Jimmy left for the conference and mingled with his friends, while I walked around Harvard Yard. What an extraordinary campus, so beautiful, so free, and so peaceful. There were students lying on the grass, talking or just sunning themselves. I thought of my own experience at the Sorbonne. Dreary, immense amphitheaters where the teachers never knew your name. You sat with your friends on hard benches, never meeting the other students. Our only fun was after class, where we'd meet in a café over a ham sandwich and a glass of beer, discussing world politics or Sartre's latest novel.

As I entered the conference hall, a woman was on the platform talking about the American cities and urban planning. I looked at the program and read that her name was Jane Jacobs, a journalist for *Architectural Forum* and *Fortune*. She was talking about urban renewal and how it had destroyed American cities by creating large bands of highway that were changing neighborhoods for the worst, killing small businesses. She pointed out how the immense building heights had a dehumanizing effect, their massive blank walls seeming almost hostile to the pedestrians on the sidewalks. I recalled then my own experience arriving in New York, how I felt like an ant crushed by the heights of the buildings. She added, "We need more people who care. We need to save our city centers, and stop the exodus to the suburbs." She was passionate and electrifying. She got a standing ovation. I wanted to meet her, but there were too many people. Later when I met Jimmy, I told him how much I enjoyed the woman's talk.

"We will meet her in New York, I promise. I know her husband. He is an architect and, like her, fascinating."

That night Jimmy took me to Durgin Park Restaurant, an immense place, packed with tourists like us. The restaurant had long wooden tables for communal eating. We sat next to a family with four children from Ohio. Everyone was very friendly, so different from the French. They were all excited that I was French, and questions flew at me:

"How do you like Boston?"

"Love it, it's more like Paris."

"New York?"

"More difficult to know . . . I haven't really explored it yet."

"What part of Paris do you live in? I know the Eiffel Tower and . . ."

It turned out that the father had been a soldier in the war and had visited Paris and enjoyed the visit tremendously. Here the food was different but also very exciting as Jimmy chose dishes I had never tasted before, such as a strange corn pudding, light and fluffy, more like a soufflé with a very strong taste of corn. I loved it!

"It's called Indian pudding," the woman told me. This was followed by a broiled fresh fish and scalloped potatoes. It was the first great meal I had had in United States. The next morning Jimmy took me to the Italian section in North Boston. There was an open market, he told me, like in Paris. All along the street were stands with merchants calling to customers to buy their fare: oysters piled high, smelling of the sea; clams; and large crabs.

"Can we have some now? Right here?" I asked one of the sellers who was pushing me to buy oysters. "I don't live here, but I would like to try them."

"Get yourself a lemon. I'll open some oysters for you. How about clams?"

"I never ate clams; I will try some."

"*Bella*, anything for your great eyes," he said.

I felt I was back in Italy where we lived after our marriage. There, the men compliment you at every corner, *bella* or not. I bought a lemon, and Jimmy and I ate half a dozen oysters and clams. I had never had clams on the half shell. It was a revelation. So different from oysters. You have to chew the clam. They are soft and hard at the same time, slightly salty, and so delicious. We continued our walk and stopped at a stand filled with vegetables. I recognized Swiss chard and Sorrel, but near them was a vegetable I didn't know. It had broad, waxy, blue-green leaves. Next to it was still another vegetable with dark green leaves, frilled with curly edges. "It's kale," the seller told me, handing me a large bunch. I cut a small piece and tasted it. It was spicy and bitter at the same time.

"What are these?" I asked pointing to another green vegetable.

"The blue-green one is collard greens, and this here, lady, is mustard green. Buy some and cook it with a piece of salted or smoked pork, and you will love it."

I wanted to buy some, but Jimmy said no because no one at home would eat it. I promised myself that when I had my own apartment, I would try them all. Then I saw stands with lettuces. "I hate iceburg lettuce," I told Jimmy. "I have to bring this lettuce home." I also bought large, round, purple eggplant and some green sweet peppers. The fish stand was great; there were all sorts of fish that were new to me. I would have loved to buy more, but to my disappointment Jimmy said no. "We are going back home on the train. You cannot take fish with you. It will spoil, and the whole compartment will smell."

On the train back to New York, I dreaded returning to Murray and Naima's apartment. I started to understand that Murray resented being kicked out of his room and sleeping in the maid's room. We had been staying there too long. I knew we had to move. On the train, Jimmy told me that he had an interview the next day with a firm of architects and planners who had a great reputation. "I hope I will get the job" he said. *So do I,* I thought, *so that we can afford an apartment.* I also decided that I had to take over the task of apartment hunting. Having made that firm resolution, I felt free to daydream about the vegetables I had just bought and wondered how I would prepare them.

That night I made a sort of soufflé with the kale. I thought it was delicious, but no one, not even Jimmy, said anything. I put aside my apparent failure as a cook and put all my energies into finding a home. Every morning, with *The New York Times* in hand, I walked through the city's streets looking at apartments. Jimmy had been hired as designer and planner at a firm called Mayer and Wittelsey. Meanwhile the tension in the house was becoming unbearable. Murray had refused to move back into his room. I had the feeling that he and Naima were fighting, but not only about us—they also fought about Anne, who like most mothers-in-law gave her opinion on everything that took place in that house. Dinners were hard to take; Murray barely acknowledged our presence; Naima, wanting peace above all else, was busy with the children and refused to intervene. Jimmy was lost in his own world, and I desperately tried to make conversation, so I talked about the apartments I had seen.

"I saw an apartment on a street called Bleecker. Wonderful. It's on the third floor, a walk up. Great view from the windows, and you know, the bathtub is in the kitchen. So romantic! Next to it is a great charcuterie with prosciutto, hams, sausages, and cheeses. Also there are street vendors selling vegetables and fruit. And best of all the rent is only $85 a month. I want to show it to Jimmy tomorrow. We can move in right away."

My announcement was greeted with exclamations of horror. "Bleecker Street, that's in the village and a three story walk up! The bathtub in the kitchen! Ridiculous Colette, you need a real apartment! Furthermore, it is too expensive."

Too expensive! I heard that statement every night as I would describe what I had found that day. Nothing was good enough for my mother-in-law, nothing was elegant enough for Murray, and Jimmy would smile at me and always say, "Tomorrow you will find something better." I was getting so angry with Jimmy. I tried to explain to him that we were causing strife between husband and wife and that even Maxwell, the three-year-old, was acting up because of it. Jimmy told me I was exaggerating, that things were not that bad, and that tomorrow I would find an apartment. Day after day, newspaper in hand, I went looking for a place to live. By now I had learned the bus system and could move up and down Manhattan quite easily. Lunches were a slight problem. I could not always find a Chock full o'Nuts to order my favorite sandwich. I tried a street vendor sausage and threw it in the garbage—nothing like Munich's sausage that we used to eat in the street. Eventually, I discovered a BLT, a tomato and bacon sandwich that I liked, but I had to learn to say, "No mayonnaise and on toasted rye bread." I could not eat the thin, soft white bread even toasted.

One night when Naima was out, I made artichokes stuffed with breadcrumbs and herbs, as I had learned to in Italy, and cooked them in olive oil. I thought that everyone would be happy, the tension would disappear, and I would be praised as a great cook. But no, no one said anything, not a word. I looked at Jimmy, who wore his far away look I now knew so well. It meant that he was thinking of an architectural problem and was totally oblivious of everything around him. Suddenly, I decided to leave the house. I had enough of this family who did not talk, who seemed not to like one another.

Slowly, I got up, left the dining room, put my coat on, and waited to see if anyone noticed that I had left the table. I waited ten minutes. Nothing happened, so I left. I walked down Central Park West toward Columbus Circle. By now I knew that part of the city quite well. I sat on a bench outside the park and looked at the people walking by. I thought I had made a mistake, coming to New York. I did not like the city, I had no friends, and Jimmy did not seem to care for me as much as he did in Italy where we first lived as husband and wife. Everything I did was either criticized or dismissed. *What was I doing here?* I wondered. I am twenty-three years old, I am still young, and I must go back to Paris, find a job, and start a new life again. But I did not want to go back to the apartment. I decided I would stay on my bench until morning and then go back, pack my bags, and leave. I must have sat down there for more than an hour when suddenly I heard Jimmy's voice.

"Oh, I found you! I was so worried; I have been walking for the last two hours. Why did you leave? I was panicky. What's wrong? I don't understand what happened. Please tell me."

I looked at his face; he looked exhausted, upset, there were tears in his eyes. "I love you," he kept on repeating, hugging me. "Why did you do that?" And so I explained and talked about my loneliness: Murray and Naima, Anne and him not understanding, not listening to me. Not helping me find an apartment.

"We have been here over two months. I want my own home with you. I want to find a job. Have a real life." I told him of the apartment I had found on Sixty-eight Street and Central Park West. "It is in the back, on the second floor. It isn't great, but please can we take it and move?" Jimmy promised that the next morning we would go and see the landlord and sign a lease. We slowly walked back to the house. They had all gone to bed. I did not have to explain anything to anyone.

The next morning as promised, we went to sign the lease. The apartment had one large living room, a small bedroom overlooking a brick wall, and a small kitchen with a dinette. Jimmy did not seem too happy but said nothing. Then we ordered a bed, and a few days later we moved in. Murray and Naima were upset with us. We had not asked their advice, and they felt offended. Anne thought we should have waited for a better place. No one was happy for us except me.

A few days later my large shipping baskets arrived with my entire trousseau. Together we unpacked, and mentally I thanked my mother for the lovely towels and sheets I now had. We went to the Salvation Army and bought two dentist stools for a few dollars and a writing desk that Jimmy stripped and painted white. (Forty years later, I still have the writing desk and the stools.) I bought a vase at the Five and Ten and filled it with flowers because by now I knew where the flower shop was. I placed one basket in the dinette and covered it with one of the tablecloths I had not wanted to take. This became our dining table, and after buying some pots and pans, I was ready to play housewife and cook my first meal.

I was finally home!

><

SNAILS WITH SWISS CHARD

Wash 1 pound of Swiss chard. Cut the leaves off the stems. Set aside the leaves and finely chop them. Dice the stems. Bring a quart of water to a boil with a pinch of salt. Then add the stems and bring to a boil; turn off the heat and drain. In the same saucepan, heat 2 tablespoons of butter, add stems, and sauté for 5 minutes or until they are tender, but do not brown. Then add the leaves and sauté for 4 minutes. Remove from the heat and set aside. Meanwhile, in a skillet heat 2 tablespoons of butter. When the butter is hot, add 2 dozen large snails, sprinkle with salt and pepper, and sauté for 5 minutes, while stirring. Remove from the heat and set aside. Peel 8 garlic cloves. Place the garlic in a saucepan, cover with 1 cup of milk. Bring to a boil, lower the heat, and simmer for 5 minutes or until the garlic is cooked. Drain the garlic. In a food processor, puree the garlic with ½ cup of heavy cream. When ready to serve, add the Swiss chard to the snails and heat for 2 minutes, then add the cream sauce, mix well, and heat through. Do not boil. Serve sprinkled with chopped parsley.

Serves 4.

LAMB SHANKS WITH HARD CIDER

Marinate the 4 lamb shanks the night before. In a bowl, mix together 2 tablespoons of lemon juice with 4 tablespoons of olive oil, 2 tablespoons of soy sauce, and salt and pepper to taste. Place the lamb in a deep bowl, and add the marinade. Turn the lamb shanks several times so that they are covered with the oil mixture. Cover the bowl with foil and refrigerate overnight. Scrape, wash, and dice 2 carrots; peel and dice 3 medium size onions; peel, seed, and dice 2 tomatoes; peel and chop half a head of garlic. In a large saucepan, heat 2 tablespoons of olive oil, add the vegetables, mix well, lower the heat, and simmer for a few minutes, while stirring. Add ½ cup chicken bouillon and 2 cups of hard cider. Bring to a boil, reduce heat, and skim the top. Cook for 4 minutes. Remove from the heat, cool and refrigerate overnight. The next day, in an ovenproof saucepan, heat 2 tablespoons of olive oil. Drain lamb shanks and add to saucepan. Brown on all sides. Remove to a platter and discard the oil. Place lamb shanks back with the vegetables and broth. Sprinkle lamb with 1 tablespoon of fresh thyme. Add more broth mixed with hard cider (equal parts broth and hard cider) if necessary, as the meat should be covered. Close with a lid and bake in a preheated oven at 350° for 2½ hours. Meanwhile, peel and quarter 1 pound of small fresh turnips and 3 celery stalks. Wash and scrape 1 pound of baby carrots. Cook each vegetable separately in salted boiling water until tender, do not overcook. Drain and set aside. Remove the shanks from the saucepan. Place the cooked vegetables in a food processor and puree. Pour sauce back into saucepan, add 2 tablespoons of butter, and simmer for 3 minutes; add the shanks, carrots, turnips, celery, salt, and pepper. Heat through. Place shanks with the sauce and the vegetables in a deep serving platter, sprinkle with fresh chopped parsley, and serve.

Serves 4.

APPLE & PEAR TART

Make the dough: In a food processor, place 1¾ cups of flour with 8 tablespoons of cold butter, cut into small pieces, and a pinch of salt. Process until the mixture forms a coarse meal. In a measuring cup, mix together 1 egg with 1 tablespoon of oil and ¼ cup of ice water. Beat with a fork. Then, while the food processor is running, slowly add the oil mixture. It will form a ball. Remove and wrap it in wax paper and chill in the refrigerator for 1 hour. Butter a 9-inch pie pan. On a floured board, roll the dough. Line the pie pan with the dough and crimp the edges. Peel, core, and thinly slice 3 Macintosh apples. Peel, core, and thinly slice 3 large Anjou pears. Form concentric circles of apples and pear slices. Dot with 2 tablespoons of butter and sprinkle the top with 2 tablespoons of sugar. Bake in a 375° oven for 40 minutes. Serve with ice cream or whipped cream.

Serves 4 to 6.

ASPARAGUS WITH BOILED EGGS

For this recipe, you need to choose thick asparagus, not pencil thin ones.

With a vegetable peeler, peel 12 large asparagus and trim ends. Place the asparagus in a large skillet and cover with boiling water. Bring to a boil, lower heat to medium, and cook until tender (about 8 minutes). Drain immediately. Place the asparagus, 4 to each plate, alongside an egg cup. In a saucepan, place 4 eggs, cover with boiling water, and cook for 4½ minutes. (For this dish, the eggs should be runny.) In a small dish, place 4 tablespoons of butter. Add a few drops of truffle oil to the butter (optional). Melt butter in a microwave. Add salt and pepper to taste. Pour the butter in a small milk pitcher, being careful not to pour in the solids, which are at the bottom. Cut off the top of each egg and serve with the butter on the side. Each person pours 1 tablespoon of butter in the egg. Mix and use the egg as a sauce for the asparagus.

Serves 4.

ONION GRATINÉE

Peel 3 large sweet onions and thinly slice. In a deep skillet, heat 2 tablespoons of butter, add the onions, and sauté over a medium heat until transparent but not brown. Then add 2 quarts of strong beef stock. Simmer for 5 minutes. Correct the seasoning with salt and freshly ground pepper. Toast 8 slices of French baguette. Divide the soup among 4 ovenproof bowls. Add 2 tablespoons of grated Swiss cheese to each bowl. Top with 2 slices of toast. Place 3 thick slices of Swiss cheese on top of the toast. Dot with butter. Bake in a 375° oven until the cheese is melted and golden brown. Serve immediately.

Serves 4.

Jimmy and I as newlyweds

2

Life in New York

We settled into our small, empty apartment. We were happy, but I realized very soon that I needed to work. Everyone around me, except Naima, was working. We also needed the money. In France, I would not have worked. At that time, young, upper-middle-class women stayed home, but here in New York, it wasn't the same. Until you had children, you were expected to work. When I wrote home that I was looking for work, my mother thought it was odd and wrote, "Doesn't Jimmy make enough money to support you?" I was upset by her comments and tried to explain to her that here in New York, there was something in the air that made you want to work and so I tried to find a job.

Every morning I scanned the newspapers for help wanted ads, but the ads were for specific professions or skills, like secretaries or clerks, and I did not know what I could do or what to look for. My degree in literature was really no help. I spoke English fairly well but could not spell or type. I had one letter of recommendation from an Italian businessman who headed an import/export company in Udine, Italy, where we had lived for a year. He had hired me hoping I would make a good secretary but fired me within a week telling me that I was totally inept. He wanted me to leave without any fuss, so he offered to give me a strong letter of recommendation. This was the extent of my working experience. I was getting quite desperate and was about to look for a job as a saleslady or babysitter, when my eye caught a small ad for someone who could write in French and in English. I quickly called and set up an appointment.

The office of Monsieur Ribaud was on Fifth Avenue near Forty-seventh Street in a building called The Fuller Building. Located at the end of a long corridor, his office was a tiny dark room with two desks, a typewriter, and a teletype machine. M. Ribaud was short, slightly bald, with his few black hairs held in place with some sort of grease. His shifty eyes were hidden behind thick-rimmed glasses, and he wore a shiny gray suit with a shirt whose collar needed ironing. He had a heavy Belgian accent, and I tried not to smile when he inquired about my French skills and my working credentials. With some hesitation, I handed him my Italian letter of recommendation. To my relief, he barely glanced at the letter and proceeded to explain that my job would be to read all of New York's newspapers every day. On Fridays I was to write a piece in French, summing up the most interesting articles I had read, and then send it by teletype to his newspaper, *La Libre Belgique,* in Brussels. I would be required to be in the office from 9:00 A.M. to 2:00 P.M. every day and answer the phone, and for this, I would be paid $35 a week, twice a month. I immediately said yes, overjoyed to have a job. I was then handed a key, and I promised that I would be on time the next day. I called Jimmy and said excitedly, "I have a real job!"

The next morning Jimmy walked me to the subway, explaining what station to exit. I looked for my station, but I must have missed it because twenty minutes later, I found myself in Queens. I got out of the train and tried to ask how to go back to Manhattan. I did not understand what my would-be rescuers were saying to me: "You can take the IRT or the BMT to go back to Manhattan."

What did these letters mean? I did not know what to do and ended on a bench, crying. I was lost, totally lost. As I sat on that bench, forlorn and thinking that I would be fired, an older man approached me and asked if I needed help. As I explained through my tears what had happened, he laughed and told me he would take me back to the Forty-second Street station. I learned in the subway that his name was Renaldo Butoni, he was an Italian journalist attached to the United Nations, and he lived in Queens. When he left me in front of The Fuller Building, he handed me his card and said he hoped we would see each other again, but not on a subway platform. Later, Renaldo and I would become quite good friends, and he would often help me in my work.

As I reached my office, I tried to imagine what excuse I could give M. Ribaud. To my astonishment the office was empty. On my desk were six newspapers, *The New York Times, The Wall Street Journal, The Daily News, The New York Post, The Sun,* and *The Herald Tribune* and instructions on how to teletype the article I would write on Friday morning. The note also said that he would come by on the fifteenth of the month to pay me. M. Ribaud kept his promise, only showing up twice a month, promptly at 9:00 A.M., staying just long enough to hand me my bimonthly check. I never found out if he or the paper liked my work or what he did the rest of the time. I was always alone in the office with my newspapers and a pair of scissors.

On the first day, I started to read *The New York Times*. I had problems with the political articles, since I wasn't familiar with the workings of political parties or the government, so I turned to the local news, which was also quite a mystery to me. Robert Wagner Jr. was then mayor of New York. There were articles about corruption, others about a mysterious Boss named Carmen DeSapio. *Who is this "Boss?"* I wondered. Since I had to wait until the evening to ask Jimmy, I went on to read the next story. This was an article about a controversy on Robert Moses's plans to build more public housing downtown. I doubted that Brussels would be interested, so I turned to the entertainment pages and read about Carnegie Hall and Mayor Wagner's hope to rescue it from demolition. Musicians and composers all over the country and abroad were gathering forces to protest its imminent destruction. This article was cut and stacked away. I read about Mayor Wagner's decision to create a free Shakespeare theater in Central Park. Again this article was cut and put away. On Friday, I would write an article incorporating all the tidbits I had read. By 12:30 P.M., it was time for lunch, and I went to explore Fifth Avenue.

Forty-second Street was lined with cafeterias and coffee houses. *Which one to choose?* They all seemed the same to me. I read their menus and wondered what could I eat. *What is a Triple Decker?* Finally, I chose a restaurant that did not look too intimidating and sat down at a small table. I ordered a hamburger but could not remember how to say rare, and I was presented with a gray, overcooked hamburger, topped with a slice of orange cheese and sweet pickles; it looked and tasted like rubber. I discovered that beyond American coffee, which I disliked, and Coca-Cola, which I found sickeningly sweet, I could not order a glass of wine nor could I ask for a beer. Unable to eat, I paid and left the place, promising myself that from then on to bring my own lunch to work.

Back at the office, I switched newspapers and turned to *The Wall Street Journal*. Scanning the front page, it was there that I caught a glimpse of American life outside of New York. For instance, there was a column about a New England woman who had started a business raising Newfoundland dogs and knitting jackets with their hair. The article was fascinating because it was bizarre and also because the woman was so successful. I cut out the article and added it to my pile. For the next few weeks when I came into the office in the morning, I first turned to *The Wall Street Journal* for its stories on small businesses. They were always fascinating vignettes and, to me, so American. I could combine them with other articles to send to Brussels on Fridays. No one ever complained in Brussels that what I wrote was often strange or far-fetched. Once in a while, I would insert important political news stories. National elections were to take place the following November, so I looked for some extraordinary events such as the controversy around Adlai Stevenson's shoes. Stevenson was the Democratic candidate for president, and the sole of one of his shoes had a hole. The embarrassing photograph was shown on the front page of *The New York Times*. Later, I found out that it may have been planted by Stevenson's people.

I enjoyed my work immensely because every day I learned something not only about New York but also about the rest of the country. Slowly, I began to understand American politics and the workings of New York City.

New York life fascinated me, especially Greenwich Village. Very often after work, I would take the subway and get off at the Eighth Street station and walk through the neighborhood. It was late June, and along the narrow curving streets, the lovely town houses had geraniums in window boxes and flowers everywhere. I spent my afternoons looking at the small funky boutiques, sitting in coffee houses, or spending hours at the Sheridan Square bookstore. On weekends, Jimmy and I would go listen to jazz or attend an avant-garde play. We often went to the first in-the-round theater in New York, the Circle in the Square Theater. I can still remember how enthralled I was to see Jason Robards in *The Iceman Cometh* or Truman Capote's *The Grass Harp*. The crowd was young like us, and after the play or the concert, we would walk to Tenth Street to the Ninth Circle for a drink or dinner or stop on Cornelia Street for a cappuccino at Caffe Cino. It seemed to me that people all around me were adventurous, that they were open to new ideas and very involved. I felt that there was hope and excitement in the air and found the city vibrant and alive. For me, the Village was a bit like the Left Bank in Paris; it felt like home.

Every morning, I looked forward to going to work. I was no longer afraid of getting lost in the subway. The only problem I had to solve was my lunch. Every day after work, I went shopping for food in our neighborhood. I found supermarket displays baffling, the food was always wrapped in plastic. For example, if I wanted to buy beef or lamb, the cuts of meat were different from the French ones, and it took many tries before I knew which one to buy. Bread was also a problem until I found a delicatessen store that sold rye bread, which was far tastier than the sliced white bread from the supermarket. I also discovered that New Yorkers liked smoked salmon and that it was as good as what I used to buy in charcuteries in Paris. I also loved Virginia ham, which is very different from the French boiled ham that I loved, slightly too sweet for my taste; but I learned that with it I still could make a very good sandwich.

Finding good vegetables and salads was also a problem. String beans seemed overgrown to me, nothing like the French haricots verts I was used to, and I hated iceburg lettuce. At first we went out to dinner, but very soon this became too expensive, so I started to cook. One night we decided to invite over for dinner Jimmy's old friend, Gabriel Sedlis, an architect from Europe who had come to the United States after the war. He had been Jimmy's classmate at Harvard. I still can remember the first dinner I prepared because I had to comb the neighborhood to find what I wanted. I made a cucumber salad with plain yogurt, garlic, and mint. Fresh mint was not easily available then in local supermarkets. I finally found a small store run by an Italian woman, who had fresh herbs growing on her windowsill. She agreed to let me have some. I also bought some chuck steak to make my own hamburgers and served them with a green peppercorn sauce; I made a puree with canned artichoke hearts using my new blender, a present from my mother-in-law. The puree was good though if too thin and slightly watery, since I had overdone the blending. But no one complained. For dessert, I made my first apple mousse, which was a great success, because I had just discovered how wonderful Macintosh apples were.

My reputation as a good but somewhat bizarre cook began with this dinner. As time went by, I became more adventurous and went beyond my westside neighborhood to shop.

One day, Jimmy announced that he had invited another old

friend from Harvard for lunch the following Saturday. "Don't make anything too French or too strange," he said. "I haven't seen him in several years, and I don't really know what he is like." *Not too French?* I decided to make an omelet, a salad, and a cake for dessert. I had been attracted by boxes of luscious cake mixes and learned that you could make a cake by just adding water and baking it in the oven. And so I started with the cake. When the cake came out of the oven, it looked nothing like the picture on the box. I had not understood the directions and had ended up baking the chocolate glaze and using the cake mix as the glaze. That cake ended up in the garbage can. As I prepared the omelet, I remembered Jimmy's request. I decided, that to make it not too French, I would add some ketchup, which would give it an authentic American touch. The friend was charming, but the lunch was an unforgettable disaster. When I brought the "American" omelet to the table, Jimmy looked astonished as he stared at the disgusting grayish-orange mass. Not knowing what to do, I immediately started to talk about my total lack of cooking experience, hoping that Jimmy's friend would forgive the horrible meal. The friend smiled as he played with his food. Jimmy looked grim, and as I was getting more and more nervous, I endlessly chattered away. As he was about to leave, he looked at me and said that he hoped I would enjoy discovering New York's restaurants. We never saw that friend again, and Jimmy made me promise to never attempt to make what I thought were American dishes.

During the week, we ate simply, shopping only at our local supermarket, but on weekends, we explored downtown and the Lower East Side. Our first stop was often the Essex Street market. The market was alive and bustling with people. The meat stands were run by Italian butchers. There I was able to find fresh chickens, rabbits, lamb, and cuts of beef or veal I could recognize. The vegetable stands offered at least three types of salads green, and I could satisfy my desires for a tender lettuce (which I learned very quickly was called Boston lettuce, reaffirming my strong belief that Boston knew good food) or escarole. There were bright red tomatoes, fresh string beans (maybe not as thin as the French ones but still quite good), large Italian eggplants, bitter sorrel, and broccoli. I often bought broccoli in attempts to prepare this uninspiring vegetable in a more imaginative way. With the broccoli, I made soufflé, tried it in a soup with turnips, or served it steamed and drizzled with olive oil bought in Little Italy. It took me much longer to be adventurous enough to buy fish because I could not recognize any except gray sole. I also explored Jewish stores on Houston Street. There I found fresh bread, fresh or baked farmer's cheese, heavy cream, and dried fruit. What I liked best was the butter. On the counter was a hill of bright yellow butter just like in France. The butter was sweet and creamy, so much better than the package variety sold in my supermarket. The saleslady would cut the butter with a wire to exactly the amount I needed. Then Jimmy and I would stop at Gus's pickle store on Essex Street and Grand Street and buy a quart of sour cucumber pickles. They were so crunchy and so garlicky that I could not resist the temptation and ate most of them on the way home. Nearby was a store that sold bagels and bialys. Jimmy had introduced me to my first bialy. I loved the hot, fresh, chewy bread with its chopped onion center. I would buy dozens and have them slathered with butter for breakfast.

Then we would walk to Katz's delicatessen for lunch. The restaurant was like nothing I had ever experienced. At lunch it was packed with people who, I was told, came from all over the city to eat pastrami sandwiches, which I disliked, or steamed corned beef, sausages, or brisket, which I loved. Along the wall was a small army of men carving the meats. I adored the thick, fatty sandwiches of steamed beef brisket. My favorite moment was standing at the counter, mouth watering, famished, watching the old man carve the brisket with such dexterity and rapid movements that I was totally mesmerized. Smiling, he would always offer me a thin slice of hot, fatty brisket for my approval. I would say "Great! Delicious!" and my sandwich would be so thick and moist that the bread would invariably fall apart. It was so succulent that I picked up the pieces with my fingers. Full and satisfied, we would find our way to Bleecker Street.

On Saturdays, Bleecker Street was lined with carts piled high with salads, two or three types of eggplants, leeks, or green peppers. Along the street, we stopped at Italian stores offering salamis, hams, cheese, fresh Parmesan, and what I liked most, sweet Italian sausages that I would serve the next day for lunch with sautéed green peppers. There were several bakeries with crisp Italian baguettes that were not as good as the French bread I was used to, but certainly a great improvement on the soft white bread from the supermarket. Back at our apartment, I would cook dinner with the things I had bought: I would make a potato and leek soup, stuffed chicken with garlic, and steamed fresh spinach. But what I liked to do on weekends was to bake those large Idaho potatoes. I was then in love with this quintessential American way of preparing a potato. But to be different, I would often top them with herb butter or fresh ricotta from Bleecker Street. In the evening we would stroll on Broadway and often go to the Thalia, a petite avant-garde movie house that showed foreign films.

My tranquil routine at work lasted only a few months. An international crisis was looming. Everything changed suddenly.

The United Nations was in full session to examine the Middle East crisis after Egypt and its leader, Nasser, nationalized the Suez Canal. The French and the English attacked Egypt; the Soviet Union sided with Egypt, and the UN Security Council called an emergency meeting of the General Assembly to discuss the problem. I was quite worried as I still had some family members living in Cairo. M. Ribaud reappeared in my life, arriving in the office in his rumpled suit, saying that from now on and for the duration of the General Assembly meetings, I was to attend UN General Assembly and Security Council meetings and write daily reports for *La Libre Belgique*. He would take my place and write the weekly article to send home. I called on Renaldo, my Italian journalist friend, to help me through the labyrinth of the United Nations. Every day for several weeks, I sat and listened to arguments on both sides. At lunchtime, Renaldo and I would stroll to a small Italian restaurant not far from the United Nations where I would order a plate of spaghetti Bolognese or veal scaloppini with clams and a glass of red wine. Sleepily, I would go back to the General Assembly meetings and doze off because of my lunch while listening to the Israeli-French arguments and the Soviet Union response. Often, the sessions would last late into the night, and I would not come home until the wee hours of the morning. Jimmy did not like coming home to a dark house and no dinner. We argued a lot about this new development, but I was so excited and interested that in the end he accepted the situation. Then when the UN sessions ended, I went back to my old routine of reading my daily newspapers.

M. Ribaud reappeared a few weeks later to announce that a Belgian state senator was arriving in New York. The senator needed a translator to accompany him to Washington, since he had important business to discuss with members of the American government. M. Ribaud offered me the job and said that I would be paid $100 a day, for three days, a lot of money for us, plus my usual salary of $35 a week. This was my first trip to Washington, and I was told that the senator would put me up in a nice hotel. Worried about me being alone with the senator, Jimmy reluctantly let me go, making me promise that I would call every day.

Senator S. was a tall, portly man, dressed in a gray pin-striped suit, shiny black shoes, and a red handkerchief in his left pocket. He looked more like an actor playing the role of a senator than a real one, but I was quite impressed. During the train ride to Washington, he explained that I was to help him secure an appointment with the newly appointed Secretary of State, Christian Herter. Senator S. knew how to reach him. The American Consulate in Brussels, who was his friend, had given him several telephone numbers. We checked in the hotel, and as Senator S. had no address in New York, he suggested that he use mine. As soon as we were registered, I started to make inquiries and quickly found that one did not get such an appointment that easily, even if you were a senator from a friendly but small country like Belgium. I was told to call again the next day, so I convinced the senator to take me on a tour of Washington's monuments. The city delighted me with its wide avenues and its great monuments that felt so much like Paris. That night Senator S. left me alone to dine at the hotel, while he went to visit some friends. Shy and lonely, I ate in my room and spoke to Jimmy for hours, knowing that the senator would pay the bill. The next day, I tried again to set up an appointment but failed. I was about to give up when a message came. The senator could meet with the then Under Secretary of State Robert Murphy the next day. Murphy would decide if a meeting with the secretary of state was warranted. From our hotel, we walked to the State Department and were greeted by Mr. Murphy. As we sat down, I heard for the first time the reason for our trip and was asked by Senator S. to translate. Senator S. stated that he represented Belgium's right wing political party. They were very concerned with the future results of the presidential elections. They had raised a million dollars, and he was empowered to offer the money to Eisenhower's campaign for a second term. At that moment, as I looked up at Mr. Murphy, I thought that he was going to explode. He jumped up, red in the face, and told us to get out of his office, and he insisted that we never, never appear before him. Shaking and scared, I translated what Mr. Murphy had said: It was totally illegal for a foreign country to interfere in American politics. Senator S. wanted to argue, but I insisted that we leave immediately. I understood that we had made a fatal mistake. Back at the hotel, I told Senator S. that I would immediately go back to New York, as he no longer needed my services. I requested to be paid. He promised to send me a check and take care of the hotel bill. Relieved, I left for New York.

I took the next few days off, and then on the following Monday, went back to work. When I arrived at the office, I was astonished to find it totally empty. The desks and the teletype machine were gone. The superintendent of the building told me M. Ribaud had moved out, and when I called the only telephone number he had given me, I discovered it was disconnected. I called the newspaper in Brussels and was told that he had been fired three weeks ago. He had never told me, and he had left the country without paying me!

For the next few days, I scanned the employment ads looking for another job, but was not successful. I looked every day for the mail, hoping to get a check from Senator S. But nothing came. I called his hotel in Washington but was told he had checked out. I called his hotel in New York but was told they had not heard from him. I was angry and upset. I felt both men had used me. A few days later, as I was preparing dinner, the bell rang. I opened the door for two men in black suits looking stern and very official. They asked if they could come in, so I called Jimmy, who found out they were from the Federal Bureau of Investigation.

"It's the FBI. They want to talk to you. We have to let them in."

Suddenly I was afraid.

"The FBI? What is the FBI? Some sort of police?"

"Never mind, Colette; I will explain later. Just answer their questions."

They began by asking me dozens of questions. When did I meet Senator S. and M. Ribaud? Did I know that he had signed the hotel bills in Washington and New York and had given my telephone number and address as the person in charge of paying the bills? No, I did not know. I tried to explain that I had just met him, that my job was to accompany him to Washington and translate for him. I was even more frightened when I learned that he had bought an expensive fur coat in Washington with a phony check, he had gambled in underground betting places and had lost huge amounts of money, and he had given my name and address as the person in charge of his office. I was devastated and petrified. As they left, the two men implied that I could be deported and sent back to France.

That night both Jimmy and I could not sleep.

"Jimmy, what if they deport me? What a disaster! And I didn't even get my $300. If they deported me, will you come with me? Do you love me?"

I cried on his shoulder, while he tried to comfort me.

"Of course I love you. I did not know I had a criminal as a wife—much more exciting. Stop crying. The truth will come out. You were innocent. This is America; nothing could happen to you." Then he added, "I am starving! Let's eat. Let's go in the kitchen and have some French scrambled eggs."

Drying my tears, I made scrambled eggs and went to bed feeling a bit less scared.

For the next few days, we heard nothing, and no one came to our door. But on the third day, the two agents reappeared. It turned out that the Belgian ambassador in Washington had cleared me. I learned that M. Ribaud and Senator S. were both criminals and not members of any political party. The FBI apologized for scaring me and left.

Years later, when I ran for political office as a councilwoman for my neighborhood, I found out that the FBI had a dossier on me and that for a few years they had monitored my career and activities.

I was unemployed once more and began searching for jobs again. In early September, I spotted an ad for a French teacher at the Convent of the Sacred Heart on Fifth Avenue. When I was growing up in Cairo, my mother, who came from a Jewish family, had converted to Catholicism. When I was seven, she had decided that I should also be a Catholic and registered me as a boarder in the Convent of Sacred Heart in Cairo. I stayed at the convent until I was fourteen. When I saw the notice, I felt that as an alumna, I had a good chance of landing the job.

The convent occupied a magnificent old house on Fifth Avenue and Ninety-first Street. In my youth, there were two orders of nuns: the mothers, who were upper class and well educated and wore elaborate habits, and the Sisters, in simpler garb who cleaned the school and cooked. Now, two decades later, the order had changed. The Mothers' habits were different

and simpler, and there were no longer any sisters. I was interviewed by the Mother Superior and tried to play up my background as an alumna of the convent, and despite my obvious
lack of experience, was given the job. The salary was $3,500 a
year, which seemed like a fortune to me after my $35 a week. I
would teach seventh, eighth, and tenth grades. Instructed to appear at 8:30 A.M., I would attend the general meeting and
morning prayers, then teach my classes. Lunch was served at
12:30 P.M., and classes would resume at 2:00 P.M. I had several
free periods during which I could sit at my desk in the teacher's
room and prepare for my classes. I was handed a weekly plan
book and told that the mother in charge of the studies would
look at my book from time to time. "One more thing," the
Mother Superior added, "we have a very important marching
band, and we compete in Cardinal Spellman's marching band
competition, and this year we want to win. If you have students
in your classes that belong to the team, their practice takes
precedent over French lessons." (As far as I know, during my
tenure at the convent, they never won.) And so my career as a
French teacher began.

I quickly discovered that I loved teaching and was good at it,
but I had problems with the nun in charge of studies. She would
pop in on my classes just as I would be telling a story about
Paris or writing a funny rhyme on the blackboard. She thought
my plan book was far too disorderly. She also thought that I told
too many stories in class, my method of teaching lacked disci-
pline, and worst of all, I did not follow the curriculum. I did attempt to change the way I taught and to follow her directives,
but soon I became bored with the planned lessons. To my mind,
making the learning of language fun was more important than
her strict teaching rules. I continued to tell stories about growing up in Paris, sing songs, and play games. Often, I had nothing

to do because most of my students were part of the marching band and rehearsals took them away. The students were, for the most part, children of wealthy Catholic New Yorkers. I learned from the other lay teachers that the majority of the students would end up next door at the Duchesne School, the convent's finishing school, and not go on to college. Those who did go on to college usually went to Marymount, a Catholic university. At my first parent-teachers meeting, I was relieved to find out that my students loved their French class and parents were very pleased with my performance. At Christmas time, I was showered with gifts. There were bottles of French perfume, scarves, leather gloves, but most of all, box after box of expensive writing paper from Tiffany & Co. (you must often write home to France, explained one of my students, upon giving me yet another box of writing paper). So for the next two years, I had a sizeable credit at the store but never quite enough to buy myself a nice Tiffany bauble.

Anne, who lived alone during the winter in Coral Gables, Florida, asked us to join her for the holidays. Jimmy, who for a while had gone to school in the South, wanted to show me Florida and see old friends. Christmas had always been very important to me. At boarding school in Cairo, I would wait impatiently for Christmas vacation hoping to see my mother, who I seldom saw, and spending some days with my grandparents, who I loved. Most Christmases, my mother would forget that I was on vacation, or she would be traveling somewhere. But my grandmother, knowing how disappointed I would be, showered me with gifts. Waking up in the morning, I would run into our large salon and there, in a corner, would be a pile of presents: books, games, dresses, lovely gold bangles, sweaters, and many other things.

I wanted to make our first Christmas in New York special.

We decided to spend Christmas Eve together in our house in New York, then the next day, we would fly to Florida to visit Anne. I bought a small Christmas tree, decorated it with just lights and placed presents all around it. Our relationship with Murray and Naima had cooled, but on weekends I often took John and Maxwell to the park. So when they asked us to join them for Christmas dinner, we accepted and postponed our trip to Florida. I offered to cook the dinner, as Naima had cooked the Thanksgiving dinner. This started a tradition that lasted for ten years. Naima and I took turns in preparing Thanksgiving and Christmas dinners. A genteel, unspoken rivalry started: who was the better cook, who had the most imagination.

For that first Christmas, I became obsessed with the dinner. I wanted to make everything special. I spent hours talking to Jimmy about it. I devised an elaborate menu. I would make a five-meat pâté to start and follow with a goose stuffed with chestnuts and apples. I would also stuff the goose's neck with the goose liver and Italian sausages, as I remembered my French grandmother doing it; prepare a carrot soufflé; and sautéed potatoes with rosemary and pine nuts. Dessert was more of a problem because I was not a very good pastry cook. I thought that caramel-poached pears would be the easiest. To find all the ingredients we needed, Jimmy and I spent the weekend before Christmas roaming the Village and the Lower East Side. We bought dried chestnuts and Italian sausages in Little Italy; for the pâté, I bought chicken breast, chopped pork, veal, and fat back in a small pork store I had found on Ninth Avenue. The goose was a problem. When I asked the local butcher for a goose, he answered that he had never sold a goose before. He said that a turkey was what normal people made for Christmas and suggested a ham as a substitution. But I thought, *I am a normal person, and I want to make goose!* I was about to give up the idea when walking down Bleecker Street, I saw a butcher shop with a sign in its window that read "Wild Game." I went in and asked about a goose. "Of course I can get you a goose," said Mr. Ottomanelli, who, along with his brothers, owned this wonderful store. "However," he added, "I'm not sure I can get a fresh one; it may have to be frozen." On the following Thursday, I proudly returned home loaded with a frozen goose, some chicken livers, and fresh herbs. This was to be my first attempt at making a goose. I had found Kosher salt, which was quite similar to the coarse sea salt my grandmother used, and, mixing it with minced garlic, I rubbed it on the goose inside and out and refrigerated the goose until Christmas. On Christmas day, I removed all the salt, slid large pieces of butter under the skin of the breast, rubbed the goose with more butter, and hoping for a golden goose, baked it in a 350° oven for four hours. It had been decided that I would prepare the rest of the dinner at my sister-in-law's house. Jimmy was to bring the goose later, close to dinnertime. I had instructed him to baste the goose from time to time and add some broth to the pan if he saw that the liquid was drying up. I then went over to my sister-in-law's house with the other ingredients. Around 7:00 P.M., I received a frantic phone call from Jimmy. He had forgotten the goose and had never basted it. It had been in the oven for over five hours, the pan looked black, and please could I rush over. The goose was cooked!

I thought I could save it and told him not to tell anyone what had happened. I cut as much meat as I could, arranged it on a platter then proceeded to make a creamy sauce with lots of butter and heavy cream, using also some of the drippings from the roasting pan. I covered the meat with the sauce, sprinkled it with chopped parsley, and brought it back to Murray's and Naima's house. The pâté was a success, and so were the soufflé and the potatoes. No one talked about the goose except to say that this was quite an original recipe. Years later, I told Naima what had happened. She laughed and said, "And we all thought you had served a very special dish from France! No one dared say it wasn't very good!"

The next day, Jimmy and I flew to Miami. In 1956, Coral Gables was a large community of mostly retired families. Anne's house, like most houses in Coral Gables, was built in the Spanish style, with a red tile roof, blue-green shutters, and ochre-stuccoed walls reminiscent of the Mediterranean. She had a lovely garden, and I was delighted to find that she had fruit trees loaded with bright large lemons, grapefruit, and limes and a jungle of banana trees. What pleased me even more was to find in the back of the house a mango tree like we had in Cairo. I had not tasted a fresh mango since I had left Cairo years ago. The sweet smelling fruit brought back memories of trips to the mango market with my Egyptian grandfather. In Cairo's market, there were many types of mangoes: some flat and round, small bright yellow ones, or very fat ones in deep purple, red, and green. Here in Florida, the red mangoes were enormous and very juicy. I sat in the garden and ate my first American mango with relish.

That night, Jimmy insisted we go to a barbeque rib restaurant on Tamiami Trail called Shorty's. "Barbecue ribs are the best thing in Florida," Jimmy explained. "You must try them, and you will find out that we have dishes here as good as anything you will find in France." The restaurant was unpretentious. The room was barn-like with wood tables and benches. Everyone sat together. In the back, there was an open pit where the ribs were slowly baked over hickory wood coals all day and all night long. We ordered several racks of ribs. The ribs were painted with a reddish-brown sauce, a mixture of tomatoes, onions, herbs, and hot spices, and when they were placed in front of me, an unexpected aroma of a winter fire, of wood burning, wafted toward me, an aroma that promised a slightly scorched but succulent meat. Grabbing a rib, I tore the meat off the bone, sauce dripping down my chin, and laughed with pleasure. The meat was tender and juicy, the best pork I had ever tasted. With the ribs, we ate steamed corn on the cob, another dish I had not had for a long time. In Cairo, the ears of corn were slowly roasted on coals. They were tough, slightly burnt; here the corn was young, tender, dripping with butter, and very sweet. With the meal, we drank large pints of ice-cold beer, and very soon, slightly drunk, we talked with everyone around us at the table. They asked the usual questions once they found out we did not live in Miami: "Where do you come from? Up North?" "No, I am French." As in Boston, I was immediately asked, "How do you like Miami?" I didn't know yet; I haven't seen anything, but I am sure I will love it. The ribs are so good!

For the next few days, we swam in the ocean and drove through Miami Beach in the evening. The hotels astonished me; they looked like bad copies of Versailles or large Renaissance castles, with towers and plaster sculptures added everywhere. They were aqua, pink, and blue, and everything was so big, so vulgar, and so exaggerated that it left me baffled. I just wanted to go back to Anne's lovely garden with the mango tree and to the incredible sandy beaches of Coral Gables.

During our stay in Florida, Jimmy and I endured a number of exasperating social occasions. One morning Anne announced that her friends at the club all invited me to lunch—

alone. *Alone? A lunch with only women?* I had never heard of it!

"Jimmy, I don't want to go. Lunch with just women! Horrible!" But Jimmy said I had to go, if just to please his mother. And so I went.

The country club resembled Cairo's country club, with its manicured lawns, a clubhouse, and a swimming pool surrounded by deck chairs and umbrellas. But what was very different was the golf course that spread far beyond the club house and was spotted with electric golf carts silently zooming around. The luncheon event was held in a private dining room overlooking the eighteenth hole. The room was full of women with white hair tinted blue, most of whom were wearing pink or light blue pantsuits. I was introduced to Ethel, who immediately handed me a box filled with a lovely white orchid. Holding the box in one hand, I did the rounds: Ethel, Sally, Molly, Rachel, Helen, names and more names swirling around me. I no longer knew who was Sally and who was Helen, but kept on hearing whispers behind my back.

"So young, so very French, what a lovely accent, like Hildegarde! Anne must be so very happy."

Finally, we found our name cards; I was placed between Anne and Ethel, and we all sat down. It was then that I made my first mistake. I opened my orchid box, removed the orchid, and plopped it in my glass of water to cries of astonishment and horror of my host, who was sitting next to me. "This is a corsage. You must pin the orchid on your dress," she said. "Don't put it in the water!" I apologized, removed the dripping orchid, and pinned it to my dress just above my breast. Very soon my dress around my breast was soaking wet, and I looked ridiculous. I unpinned it, placed it next to my plate, smiled, and since all the women were looking at me, attacked the first course: large, chilled, boiled shrimps surrounded by a familiar pink, slightly sweet cocktail sauce. I tried to talk about New York, and my experiences at work, but no one really was listening. They were more interested in local gossip: which widow was flirting with whom and who was giving a party for New Year's, what to wear, etc. Anne whispered that Ethel was giving a very lavish New Year's party and that we were invited but not everyone at the table was. The next course came along, and Ethel, to everyone's approval, announced loudly that she had ordered the course in my honor: chicken cordon bleu. I looked down at my plate. Lying there was a piece of chicken breast topped with what looked to me to be ham and covered with a beige, slightly gelatinous sauce. As I took a bite, all eyes were on me. To my mother-in-law's dismay, I said in a very loud voice, "It is quite good, but it is not French." Utter silence followed my statement, and I realized then that I had made another major mistake. Trying to save the moment, Anne changed the subject, saying that I had spent most of my childhood in Egypt and probably did not know French cuisine too well. From their looks, I knew that now Anne had made a mistake. I was no longer this lovely French girl but some strange Egyptian creature. I could see in their faces what they were thinking: "Poor Anne, look what she got. A strange foreigner; an Egyptian at that . . . she must be so upset." I tried to save the situation as the dessert, a rich chocolate cake was placed in front of me; I exclaimed in the most French accent I could muster that this was the best cake I had ever had. But the damage was done. Nobody cared!

New Year's Eve was yet another trial. I dressed very carefully and told Jimmy I was afraid of the luncheon guests who would be coming, but he just laughed and said they would have all forgotten about me, and Anne added that it was a privilege to be invited and that not all of her friends were.

"You are going to have a lovely time. The food there is always delicious." I thought of my lunch and sighed in despair. Jimmy laughed at my sad face and said, "Come on, Colette. It won't be so bad! Cheer up; we are going together. It will be fun."

The house was an immense pink stucco house with red Spanish roof tiles, arches, and a lovely patio with a fountain in the center. Women wore long flowing dresses, and men wore suits in iridescent dark blue or white jackets. Again I was introduced as Anne's new French daughter-in-law. Very soon I was surrounded by several men, all talking at the same time. I heard them whisper: "You know Frenchmen are lazy; they take two hours for lunch. Also when you visit Paris and they spot you as a foreigner, they raise their prices. You cannot bargain with them. After all, they forgot that we liberated them." Someone added, "All Frenchmen are drunks; they drink wine all the time . . . even for breakfast!" It was an avalanche of criticism that astonished me. I was about to respond when one man, slightly drunk, added that he was eagerly waiting for midnight to kiss me, "What a treat! A real French girl!" and everyone agreed and thought it was a great thing to do. At that point, upset and on the verge of tears, I went to look for Jimmy. "Take me home. I hate it here. Please take me home. . . ."

And so we left. Back at the house, we made a fire in the fireplace, and Jimmy tried to comfort me. As midnight approached, Jimmy kissed me and whispered, "Happy New Year in your new country. Let's make love in front of the fire, and let's make a baby . . ."

The next morning I knew something in me had changed: My breasts felt rounder. I felt full and very happy—sure that I was expecting a child. Anne had been quite upset by our departure, but Jimmy explained that everything was so new for me that I had felt homesick for Paris. She accepted his explanation and forgave me.

A few months later, I discovered that I was indeed pregnant. We decided that we needed a larger apartment so we moved to a two-bedroom apartment on Sixty-eighth Street, near Central Park West, with the same small dinette but a large living room and windows that overlooked the street. We bought some furniture, a couch, two chairs, and a dinette. The large wicker baskets were put away; we were ready to invite our new friends for dinner. We invited Gabriel Sedlis and his girlfriend; Peter Greenquist, a young man who had gone to Europe with Jimmy in 1949 and was working in a publishing house; and Michael Brill and his wife, Judy. Michael, an architect like Jimmy, was funny and very fat. He loved food, and it was amusing to cook for him. That night I went all out. I prepared a choucroute garnie, a French sauerkraut dish cooked in champagne with sausages, smoked ham, and boiled potatoes served with French mustard. With it I served hot Italian baguettes and fennel salad. The guests oohed and aahed and said they never tasted such delicious sauerkraut. I had found the sauerkraut in the Lower East Side, the sausages Uptown in the Eighties in a German neighborhood, and the fennel in Little Italy. We drank lots of wine, talked about politics, the state of architecture, the future, and what a great cook I was. I was proud and happy.

As I was going to bed, I thought, *This is my life; this is my home. I am going to have a baby.* For the first time in many years, I felt I belonged somewhere. I was sure that the whole world was open to me, that in New York nothing was impossible, and that I could do anything I wanted.

>≤

CUCUMBER SALAD WITH MINT

Oriental cucumber is long and narrow and has fewer seeds than the regular cucumber.

Peel and thinly slice 2 Oriental cucumbers. Place the cucumbers in a bowl. In another bowl, beat together 1½ cups of plain yogurt; add ½ teaspoon of lemon juice, and 1 tablespoon of olive oil, and 1 garlic clove, minced, and salt and pepper to taste. Mix well and pour over the cucumbers. Then chop 2 tablespoons of fresh mint leaves. Add to the salad and mix well. Refrigerate until ready to serve.

Serves 4.

HAMBURGERS WITH GREENPEPPER SAUCE

Shape 1½ pounds of ground round into 4 hamburgers. In a large skillet, heat 1 tablespoon of butter with 1 tablespoon of olive oil. When the oil is hot, add the hamburgers and cook to desired doneness. Remove from the skillet and keep warm. Meanwhile, add 1 tablespoon of butter to the same skillet and scrape the sides. Add 1 small onion, thinly sliced, and sauté until the onions are transparent. Then add 1 cup of chicken broth, salt, pepper, and 1 tablespoon of green peppercorns. (These are available in jars in any gourmet store or supermarket.) Simmer for 5 minutes. Place the hamburgers on a platter, pour the sauce over them, and serve.

Serves 4.

ARTICHOKE PUREE

Drain 2 8-ounce cans of artichoke hearts. In a skillet, heat 1 table-spoon of olive oil. When the oil is hot, add the hearts, and sauté for 3 minutes. Then remove from the heat and cool. In a food processor, place the artichokes, 2 eggs, salt and pepper, 2 garlic cloves, 1 tablespoon of thyme, 1 tablespoon of flour, and ¼ cup of heavy cream. Process until all the ingredients are pureed. Return the puree to a saucepan and cook for 5 minutes, stirring all the while. Add 1 tablespoon of fresh butter at the last minute. Serve sprinkled with chopped parsley.

Serves 4.

STUFFED ARTICHOKES

In a large bowl filled with ice water, squeeze the juice of half a lemon. Using stainless steel scissors, cut the tips of 4 large arti-chokes. Place them in the bowl, and leave them there while you make the stuffing. Mix together ¼ cup of finely chopped parsley along with 2 minced garlic cloves, 2 finely minced anchovies, and the zest of 1 lemon. Mix well, then add ¼ cup of fresh bread crumbs along with 1 tablespoon of olive oil and fresh black pep-per (to taste). Drain the artichokes, and gently separate the leaves. Place about ¼ teaspoon of stuffing between the leaves. In a large saucepan, heat 2 tablespoons of olive oil. When the oil is hot, add the artichokes, browning them on all sides. Then stand the artichokes upright. Add ½ cup of strong chicken broth. Bring to a boil, lower the heat to medium, cover, and cook for 40 min-utes. Serve at room temperature.

Serves 4.

CHICKEN WITH GARLIC

This recipe is for a 3½-pound chicken. Wipe the chicken and place in a large bowl. In a small bowl, mix together 1 tablespoon of lemon juice with 2½ tablespoons of olive oil, 2 tablespoons of mushroom soy, and salt and pepper. Pour the mixture on the chicken and refrigerate for 2 hours. Meanwhile, peel a whole head of garlic. Remove the chicken from the refrigerator. Slide some garlic cloves under the skin of the breast; place a handful of cloves in the cavity. Place the chicken in a roasting pan with the sauce from the marinade. Surround the chicken with the remaining garlic cloves. Add 1 cup of water to the pan and roast in a preheated 350° oven for 1 hour, basting the chicken from time to time. Remove the chicken from the oven. Carve it and place on a serving platter surrounded by the garlic cloves. Add 1 cup of chicken bouillon to the pan, heat, correct the seasoning by adding salt and pepper to taste and 1 tablespoon of fresh tarragon. Pour the sauce over the chicken and serve with roast potatoes.

Serves 4.

GOOSE WITH CHESTNUTS AND APPLES

Today one can find already peeled chestnuts, which I find easier than cooking and peeling chestnuts. Goose is often available frozen. If you can, try to find a butcher that will get you a fresh goose.

Wipe and remove as much fat as possible from a 10-pound goose. Keep the fat for the neck. Cut off the neck, setting aside the skin. Rub the goose with 1 cup of Kosher salt and refrigerate overnight uncovered. This step will help dry the skin and allow the fat to escape more freely during cooking. The next day wipe away the salt. Peel 4 garlic cloves and slice. Make incisions on the goose's skin and insert the garlic. Rub the goose with soy sauce, and sprinkle it with 3 tablespoon of dried tarragon and freshly ground pepper. Prick all over the goose's skin. Place the bird in a large roasting pan and on a rack. Add 2 cups of chicken bouillon to the roasting pan. Preheat oven 375°. Roast the goose for 15 minutes at that temperature. Then reduce the heat to 325° and cook for 4 hours. (From time to time, remove the fat from the roasting pan. Keep the fat in a jar to be used during the year for vegetables or cooking meats.) The goose is cooked when the leg moves easily. Remove the goose from the oven, and allow the bird to rest 15 minutes before carving. Degrease the juices in the roasting pan. Add 1 cup of chicken bouillon, salt and pepper, and tarragon, and simmer for 5 minutes. Serve the sauce on the side.

Serves 6.

CARROT SOUFFLÉ

Peel 6 young carrots and cut in 1-inch pieces. Place the carrots in a saucepan, cover with water, and cook for 15 to 20 minutes until the carrots are tender. Drain. Place the carrots in a food processor with 4 egg yolks, ½ cup of heavy cream, and 1 tablespoon of thyme or sage. Process until the carrots are pureed. Remove to a bowl. Beat 4 egg whites until stiff. Gently fold the egg whites into the carrot puree. Pour the mixture in an oven-proof bowl and bake in a reheated oven for 45 minutes at 375°. Serve with chicken or steak.

Serves 4 to 6.

POACHED PEARS WITH CARAMEL

Peel 4 Anjou pears. In a deep saucepan, place the pears side by side. Add 3 cups of water with 1 cup of sugar and ½ cup of raspberry jam. Bring to a boil, lower the heat, and cook for 15 minutes or until the pears are tender when pierced with a fork. Remove the pears to a serving bowl. Cook the liquid until reduced to 1 cup. Pour the juice on the pears and refrigerate. Just before serving, make the caramel. In a heavy-bottom saucepan, place 2 cups of sugar with 2 tablespoons of water and ½ tablespoon of lemon juice. Melt the mixture over low heat, stirring all the while, until the melted sugar turns a golden brown. Pour the caramel over the cold pears. Garnish with fresh mint, and serve as is or with whipped cream or vanilla ice cream.

Serves 4.

CHOUCROUTE COOKED IN CHAMPAGNE

Wash 4 pounds of sauerkraut under cold running water. In a large saucepan, cook 1 cup of cubed double smoked bacon over medium heat until well done. Add the sauerkraut and mix well. Then add 10 juniper seeds, 10 peppercorns, and ½ bottle of champagne. Mix well, lower the heat, and simmer for 1 hour, stirring from time to time. Then add a 1-pound piece of smoked bacon, 1 kielbasa cut in 3-inch pieces, 4 smoked pork chops, and simmer for another hour. Add more champagne if necessary. Five minutes before the dish is ready, boil 4 frankfurters. (These should be the real ones from Charlotte and Weber.) Serve the choucroute with boiled potatoes, plenty of French bread, and good Dijon mustard.

Serves 4.

FENNEL SOUP

Cut off the ends of 3 fennel bulbs. Quarter the fennel and place
in a large saucepan with 4 potatoes, peeled and quartered, and 1
onion, quartered. Add 3 quarts of chicken broth, bring to a boil,
lower the heat to medium, and cook until the potatoes are done
and soft. Puree the soup. Then add 2 tablespoons of butter along
with salt and pepper and 1 tablespoon of chopped mint. Heat the
soup. Pour the soup in 4 individual bowls, drop ½ tablespoon of
crème fraîche in each bowl, and garnish with dill.

Serves 4.

With Marianne, my first child

3

Exploring

❧❧

Marianne was born on September 27, 1957, on a cool autumn morning. I took a leave of absence from the convent to take care of her when suddenly, after barely two months, I received a frantic call. My replacement was a disaster. The students hated her, and parents were complaining. Could I come back sooner? I was breast-feeding Marianne and enjoying being a mother, and the prospect of teaching again so soon did not appeal to me. But we needed the money, and when Mother Superior said that my schedule would be changed to allow me to return home at noon to feed the baby, I accepted. It was then that I was faced with a big problem: I needed a baby-sitter. All the ones that I interviewed were very expensive; we could not afford them since we had very little money. I put an ad in the local neighborhood paper, and Frau Zeimnitz came into our lives.

A Viennese woman living in the United States for over thirty years, Frau Zeimnitz had been a governess for wealthy Upper East Side families. She was married but had no children, and I never did meet Herr Zeimnitz. Now retired, she was bored and missed looking after children. The Fraulein was a short, bosomy woman and looked something like an oversized keg of beer. She was in her late sixties and wore a drab gray suit that matched her hair. I was slightly frightened of her and wondered if I should let her take care of my baby. But I had no choice. "I can pay $35 a week," I explained, "and you have to be here promptly at 9:00 A.M. and stay 'til 3:30 P.M." This was, even at that time, a miniscule salary. I was sure she was going to refuse, and I would have an excuse not to go back to work. Instead she answered in an imperious voice: "Show me the baby!"

We went into Marianne's room to look at the tiny sleeping baby. Marianne opened her eyes, smiled, and went back to her dreaming. Fraulein scowled, looked around, and barked, "Where is the carriage? And where are her clothes?"

And so I knew then that Fraulein was here to stay. I showed her Marianne's dainty knitted dresses that my mother, who was in Paris, had so lovingly made, the sheets with embroidered blue jumping rabbits and the ones with pink dancing elephants, both of which I had never used. I explained that my mother had copied Princess Grace of Monaco's child's trousseau, hoping that her first grandchild would be as well dressed. With a cluck of her tongue, Fraulein approved.

My Uncle Clement had sent me an enormous classic English carriage that I disliked because it was, for my taste, too ostentatious. On seeing the large, imposing-deep-blue lacquered carriage with its matching blue canopy embroidered with Marianne's initials, Fraulein's tongue clucked furiously like a hen that had just laid the perfect egg. I realized that I had nothing to fear and could go back to work without worrying about my daughter.

The year went by without incident, and I was rather naively unaware of what was going on around me. My life gravitated around Jimmy, my child, and my teaching. I was getting used to New York, we had new friends, and my English was quickly improving. On weekends, Jimmy and I would take Marianne for walks in Central Park or explore other parts of the city. We would stroll down Mulberry Street, through the heart of Little Italy. Mulberry Street was lined with Italian restaurants. We would stop for an Italian espresso and a piece of torrone at Ferrara's on Grand Street. Sometimes we'd shop at Di Paolo, a grocery store packed with salamis, hams, mozzarella, and cans of imported tomatoes. I would try my Italian with the owner's son while he thinly sliced some prosciutto or compared the different pecorino cheeses that were displayed on the counter. While Jimmy and I walked home, laden with Italian goodies, I tried to imagine what I was going to cook that night: maybe spaghetti with fresh tomatoes and mozzarella or veal chops covered with a layer of pecorino.

Although I was teaching, my salary was not high enough to complement what Jimmy was earning. We were always broke. I wondered what else I could do. I placed an ad in *The New York Times,* offering my services for translation work. I received many calls and got an assignment to translate business documents for a bank. The documents were technical and boring; however, I was learning how to write in English. I used to work late at night while Marianne slept, and Jimmy worked late in the office. It was during this period that Jimmy's office called to say that he had had an accident and was in the emergency room at New York Eye and Ear Infirmary. Someone had thrown an eraser, and it hit his eye and tore his cornea.

When I got to the hospital, I was sent to the intensive care unit. I waited for the doctors to let me in, and when I was finally able to see Jimmy, I was terrified: Both his eyes were bandaged. *Was he blind?* A young Chinese doctor was standing next to him. As I bent down to kiss him and hold his hand, he whispered to me: "Colette, I am so scared. These eyes are my life. What will happen if I can't see? What will I do?" I turned to the doctor.

"I am Doctor Chen, Suzanne Chen," she said. "He will be fine. His cornea was torn but not badly. He will heal, but it may take weeks. We will keep him here. I will look after him. Please don't worry, and tell him not to worry. I promise: He will see, but he has to rest and keep his eyes closed. We have to prevent his eyes from moving so the wound heals faster."

I looked at Jimmy again. He looked sad lying there with his head on the pillow, his eyes covered by two heavy bandages. Several times as she turned to leave, she repeated, "Don't worry; he will be fine. I will see him later."

"You will be all right. I like her; she would not lie. Please don't worry. I will be here with you. I will read to you and stay next to you. It is just a week until you come home."

That afternoon, I stayed with Jimmy then went home to reorganize my life. I would need a baby-sitter every day after Frau Zeimnitz went home. I would have to organize my classes so I could run to the hospital and see him at lunch and then again at dinner. The nuns were very kind and allowed me to switch my classes so I could be free at noon. Frau Zeimnitz agreed to stay until after dinner so that I could spend some time with Jimmy.

Doctor Chen came to see Jimmy several times a day and chatted with him. She was a beautiful young woman, thin, petite with straight dark black hair and a wonderful warm smile. Together they talked about China and her family. I thought it strange that she spent so much time with Jimmy. *Was I jealous?* Maybe, but I resolved to befriend her.

I learned that Dr. Chen was born in Shanghai. But at the age of two, she had escaped with her parents to Hong Kong, fleeing the Japanese invasion. When she was twelve, as China became communist, she was sent to her mother's family in New York to attend school. At a very young age, she became interested in becoming a doctor. Her parents and her two brothers came over to America much later. One was an architect who worked for a firm that Jimmy knew. Doctor and patient talked about architecture, politics, and food. Food at the hospital, as expected, was horrendous. So every day I cooked something to bring for Jimmy's lunch then returned home and cooked his dinner. But what do you cook for someone who is bored, lying in bed, his eyes closed, having nothing to do but listen to music and eat? The food had to smell good and taste even better. This was quite a challenge. I bought a hot plate, so I could reheat some of the dishes I brought. I roasted a chicken and served it room temperature with a cold tomato sauce; on another day, I served it with a spinach and tarragon sauce. I made a sweetbread salad with raw mushrooms and julienne fennel, and I poached salmon and served a green mayonnaise to go with it. I grilled sliced eggplant served with lemon vinaigrette and made his favorite, a meatloaf with pork, veal, and beef, which he could eat cold the next day. At every meal, Jimmy insisted we play a game. I was to describe what was on the plate, the color, the texture of the food I was about to serve him, and how it was arranged. Then he would describe the taste as he bit into a piece of chicken or fish. It was through playing this game that I learned to talk about food in vivid language and describe a dish so well that, as Jimmy told me later, he could see it.

Ten days later, Jimmy was discharged with one eye still bandaged. Dr. Chen proposed coming to the house regularly to see how he was doing. Jimmy was quite pleased with this arrangement. I, on the contrary, thought, *Was all this personal attention unusual?* I did not know, but I decided that the best way was to please Jimmy. I invited her for dinner the following week. Over dinner, we talked about food, culture, and Chinese customs. It was a wonderful evening, and suddenly I did not mind that she took such interest in Jimmy. From then on, she came at least once a week to look at his eye, which was healing, and to have dinner. She always came with some new ingredients: a sauce, a Chinese vegetable, or some strange candy for Marianne. She would talk about architecture and Chinese politics with Jimmy and about her family and food with me.

One Sunday, I received a phone call from Suzanne inviting me to go shopping with her in Chinatown. I jumped at the opportunity. Jimmy and I used to go shopping in Chinatown, but beyond buying fresh fish and fruit, we did not venture very far. To go with Suzanne would be a great adventure. And so one Sunday morning in February, Suzanne and I went down to Chinatown.

Chinatown then was not as spread out as it is today. It was a small triangle of streets bordered by Canal Street, the Bowery, and Worth Street. Its main shopping streets were Mulberry and Mott. The restaurants were around there, but also on the little crooked streets: Elizabeth, Pell, and Baxter. The streets were teaming with people buying food for the holidays, since the Chinese New Year was only a few days away. As we passed some restaurants, delicious aromas invaded the street. I was famished although it was just 10:00 A.M.

Looking at me, Suzanne could tell I wanted to eat something and suggested we have a bite before starting on our shopping adventure.

"Follow me; I know a small dim sum place on Baxter Street. The dim sum is Cantonese and really fresh."

I had had dim sum with Jimmy before, but we always went to a Chinese restaurant where *Genjis* (foreigners) went, never to an all-Chinese place. The restaurant, located on Baxter Street, was jammed with people, eating and wildly chatting. Young Chinese women were pushing steaming carts from table to table, chanting the names of the foods they hawked. Suzanne knew the owner, so we immediately got two seats at a big round table with eight others. She stopped the first cart and chose three different steamed dumplings, then from another cart chose what looked like a large white noodle stuffed with shrimps. As the third cart approached, I saw chicken feet.

"Can we have some of these?"

"You like chicken feet? Americans never eat them."

"I am French. When I was a child, my grandmother made soup with chicken feet. We would eat them with coarse salt. I loved them."

First, Suzanne taught me how to use chopsticks and served me my first dumpling. The dumpling skin was very thin, translucent, and was stuffed with bits of shrimp and pork. The dumplings were served with a light soy sauce and julienned ginger. Delicious! Then came small, round, steamed dumplings.

"Pick them up with your spoon and be careful; they are full of broth."

The dumpling squirted hot broth into my mouth. The broth was spicy, and the dumplings had chopped pork, bits of mushroom, and ginger. Simply luscious! I could have eaten a dozen. The third dumpling was vegetarian filled with minced spinach, chopped scallions, and peanuts. Fantastic! I tried the wide noodles stuffed with shrimps. They were like a very white, thin crêpe filled with shrimps and steamed; they were served with a light soy sauce. Its bland taste was in complete contrast to the crunchy, spicy ginger-coated shrimps. Then I attacked the chicken feet.

They were totally different from my grandmother's boiled chicken feet. These tender, golden-brown feet were cooked in a sweet soy sauce. They were soft on the outside with crunchy centers. I was in heaven; I never tasted anything so wonderful. We then had lightly fried Hakka-style stuffed tofu. Suzanne explained that each Chinese province had a different cooking tradition. Hakka food, which she loved ever since her stay in Hong Kong, came from the north of China. Their cuisine, she said, was a mixture of sea and land: fish, seafood, pork, and chicken. The simple triangles of tofu were stuffed with dried shrimp and cubed pepper, then lightly fried. Very different from the steamed dumplings we had just tasted, less spicy but far richer.

Later as we walked toward Mulberry Street, Suzanne said we were going to Mott Street to pick up a live fish.

"At New Years, you must always serve a steamed 'live fish,' head and tail. The fish brings good luck to the family."

The fish store had a giant tank near the window filled with a variety of fish I had never seen before. Large black ones with whiskers, small fish that looked like dorade, or silver fish. Suzanne asked for a large fighting fish. The man who was helping us picked up a net and looked first at the fish in the tank. He pointed at a large black fish that was swimming swiftly. Suzanne agreed, and the man placed the fish in a large plastic bag. The fish was really fighting, hitting his tail against the bag. We both laughed; this was a true fighting fish.

We then walked down the street to a large grocery store that sold vegetables, meat, and poultry. Outside the store were bins filled with several Chinese mushrooms. Some of them had cracked caps showing white streaks. These, Suzanne told me, were more expensive than those with regular brown caps. The cheaper kind was for soups, and the expensive kind was used in main courses with Chinese broccoli or with sautéed chicken. The expensive ones would very soon become my favorite, as I learned how to soak them for several hours to make a delicious mushroom consommé. Suzanne then pointed to some dried yellow sticks, which she explained were dried bean curd that could, after being soaked in water for an hour, be transformed into knots and added to stews. From that day on I added them to my Boeuf Bourgignon, which would never again be the same.

We bought cellophane noodles and three sorts of soy sauce; the mushroom dark soy would also become a staple in my kitchen, as I used it when I roasted a chicken or marinated quails or fish. We also picked up dried snow fungus that looked like a dried white chrysanthemum (they don't taste like much, Suzanne said, but added to any dish the fungus will absorb the fragrance of whatever is cooking), lily buds, wood ears, and cloud ear mushrooms. Then we looked at the fresh vegetables. Suzanne suggested that I first try the dark green, long string beans. "Try them with sautéed Chinese chives; they will taste very much like your own French haricot beans."

I also bought some flowering Chinese broccoli. While she chose vegetables, she would cry out their names: "This is cilantro, better but stronger than parsley. . . . This sausage-like vegetable is fresh lotus root. . . . This beautiful twisted thing is fresh ginger root. . . . This big potato is really taro root. Chinese use them in stew, or to make puree, or deep fry them."

As we walked along the poultry aisle, she pointed to a black skinned chicken. "My mother makes a broth with them whenever we have the flu. She says it makes you strong. These tiny brown eggs are from quails."

I also saw small chickens, squabs, and plump quails that I had not seen since I had left France. I told Suzanne that from now on, I would come every week and shop in Chinatown. She laughed and said I would need her to translate since very few people in

Chinatown spoke English. And so a tradition evolved where once a month I would meet Suzanne in Chinatown to shop. Jimmy would meet us later, and we would dine in one of her favorite restaurants. I learned that restaurants that catered to Chinese had two different menus: one for the Chinese in Chinese and one in English. I also learned that the strips of colored paper on the walls with Chinese writing were the specials of the day. Once we went alone to a restaurant that Suzanne had often taken us, and I asked the waiter for one of the dishes on the wall. He shook his head and said emphatically, "No," but I insisted, and so the waiter brought me a dish that looked awful. Giant worms swimming in a heavy sauce was what it resembled, and it tasted like rubber tires. I had ordered Sea Slugs! From then on, whenever we went out with Suzanne and her family, I took down the names of the dishes I liked, and Suzanne would write them in Chinese so that I would be able to spot them on the walls.

Slowly my cooking changed. I became bolder in mixing Chinese ingredients in French or American dishes. I served mushroom consommé made with Chinese mushrooms, rubbed a roast chicken with dark soy sauce, made a French puree with taro root, and served steamed spinach with sautéed lily buds. My friends would always ask before tasting, "Colette, what's that floating in my soup?" or "I like those crunchy vegetables; what are they?" I gained a reputation for being a weird but excellent cook. I also started to read about China and its culture. My dream was to visit China and experience for myself the dishes that Suzanne used to talk about but said were not available here.

On warm, sunny days, Jimmy and I would walk across the Brooklyn Bridge into Brooklyn Heights where we had friends. With them we would parade down the Promenade overlooking the East River and sit in the sun admiring the vista of skyscrapers of Lower Manhattan. I liked Brooklyn Heights with its narrow streets and lovely town houses, which reminded me more of Europe than my Upper West Side neighborhood. It was on one of our walks in Brooklyn that I discovered Atlantic Avenue and its Middle Eastern food stores. The discovery would change my life.

After leaving Egypt for Paris in 1947, I had consciously shunned my Egyptian past, desperately wanting to be French. I had worked hard at losing my singsong Egyptian accent, learned to dress like I imagined a French young woman would, and never looked back at my Egyptian past. Now being French in the United States seemed to be my passport to a better life. In New York everything French had cachet. As Jimmy and I walked past a store on Atlantic Avenue, I stopped short as I noticed a cascade of loofas hanging on a nail. *Loofas!* These were the vegetable sponges that Aisha, my maid, washed me with until my skin would be red as a lobster when I was a six-year-old girl! As I stepped into the shop—the Oriental Pastry and Grocery—the smell of cumin and coriander hit me with such force that I staggered. I was back in Cairo in the kitchen with Ahmet, sitting on the counter, eating a pita filled with warm, lemony *ful medamas* (richly braised fava beans). A smooth male voice said, "Ahlan wa sahlan." Without thinking, I repeated the familiar greeting. The words came out without my knowing that I could still speak some Arabic. I looked around at the shelves filled with food I remembered: jars of *tehina* and *tarama*, buckets of briny vine leaves, jars of rose petal jam, honey, and tiny stuffed eggplants. On the floor were barrels filled to their brims with multiple varieties of rice, small red and black lentils, dried brown beans from Egypt, and a panoply of macerating olives—pickled, cracked, oiled, and peppered. There were also pickled onions and lemons that I remembered using in stews, and my favorite, bright pink turnips pickled in beet juice and vinegar to eat with *ful*. Near the counter were baskets of fresh pita breads that I had not seen in more than ten years, and in a jar in a corner, were paper-thin sheets of apricot paste that we used to roll around ice cubes and suck like lollipops in the summertime. I wanted to buy everything. The voice I had heard belonged to a man with curly black hair and a warm smile standing behind the counter. How did he know I would understand? And did I? I thought I did, but I wasn't sure. Shy and afraid of making a mistake, I responded in English, "Why me?" *"Habibi,"* (my dear one), "you look Egyptian or Lebanese," he said laughing. I asked for a jar of *tehina,* and a pound of *ful medamas* and wondered if he had *mulukhiyya* (a bitter green herb used to make a popular soup in Egypt)? "Yes, of course . . . two kinds. You want dried or frozen?" I didn't know, but having an aversion for frozen foods, I chose dried and was handed a large bag of brittle leaves. I asked for cumin and coriander, two loofas, a pound of olives, and a container of pickled turnips. Then with a loud, happy *Ma'al-salaama* (good-bye), laden with my purchases, Jimmy and I returned home. On the way, I promised Jimmy that he would have a great dinner that night.

Back home, as I looked at all the food, I suddenly realized that I had no idea how to prepare any of it. In Cairo, no girl in my family was allowed in the kitchen. The kitchen was the cook's domain. True, I had managed to sneak in without my grandmother noticing. Ahmet, our cook who liked me, would plop me on the kitchen counter and let me taste what he was preparing. I looked, smelled, ate, but nothing more. *Tehina,* I remembered, was a light creamy sauce, not that thick oily paste I had in front of me. What should I do with this enormous bag of *mulukhiyya?* The soup I loved was a smooth, deep green soup, redolent of garlic and cumin, and served with a mound of steamed rice. How did one transform these dry leaves into that lovely soup? *Ful medamas* was served with pickles and slices of hard boiled egg. But what had made the egg whites so brown? I didn't know, but I thought that I could cook the beans and do without the eggs. I boiled the beans for two hours and tasted them. Their skins were too tough; it was nothing like the warm soft ones Ahmet would give me to taste in a fresh pita bread. That night we ended up eating pickles, olives, bread, and cheese. I promised myself that the following weekend I would go back and ask the owner of the store how to prepare the dishes I longed for.

The following weekend, I dragged Jimmy back to Atlantic Avenue. Mohammed, the owner, on seeing me again so soon, affectionately called me *sukkara* (honey, sugar) and was willing to explain everything to me. Pen and paper in hand, I took notes. He told me how to make a good *tehina,* with water and lemon juice; that dried *mulukhiyya* had to be pressed through a very fine sieve and added to strong chicken broth along with cumin, coriander and garlic; that *tarama* was mixed with soft white bread and lemon juice, and that *ful* had to be soaked overnight and slowly cooked for nearly twenty-four hours. "It is much better to buy cans of *ful.* All you have to do is heat them and mix them hot with lemon juice, olive oil, salt, and pepper."

Atlantic Avenue was like a slice of Cairo to me with all its Arab shops. There was, for example, a larger, more elegant store across the street from Oriental Pastry called Sahadi, selling foods from all over the Middle East; further down the street were two bakeries, more Syrian than Egyptian; a butcher; and one or two Yemenite restaurants. I was eager to return home and try again to cook an Egyptian dinner. The *tarama* turned out perfectly, creamy clouds of lemony caviar flavored mousse, just as I remembered. I tried to squeeze the dry *mulukheyya* leaves through a fine sieve, but my fingertips were scraped, and I decided that next time, I would buy the frozen version. Miraculously, the soup turned bright green, and its garlicky, grassy aroma summoned Jimmy to the kitchen. I had succeeded. The food was good but not quite what I remembered. Jimmy loved it. Soon I started to cook Egyptian dishes for our guests. Later I went further, remembering my grandmother and

Ahmet's other dishes, and tried from memory to reproduce exactly what Ahmet had cooked in Cairo. I made stuffed vine leaves, cooked rice the Egyptian way; I made *sanbuseck* (small pastries filled with cheese) and baked chicken on a bed of leeks. To my surprise, I had, through memory, become an expert cook of Egyptian dishes.

Something else also changed. Gradually, I began to recall with a certain pleasure small incidents from my life growing up in Cairo. I would tell Jimmy about my grandmother's poker day and how, if she won, I would get some money, or about my grandfather who took me to Cairo's mango market. I even sang Arabic songs to Marianne. From then on, I often spoke about my life in Cairo to friends. I was no longer ashamed of my past, and to everyone who asked where I came from, I now answered, "I am half French, half Egyptian," to the chagrin of Eunice Whittlesey, the wife of one of the partner's in Jimmy office. She would state in an authoritative voice, "You don't look Egyptian . . . you look French." I had a problem dealing with people like Eunice who thought of me as too loud, too Mediterranean, and probably just a bit too sexy. Jimmy tried to explain their reaction as naturally Waspish, more reserved, but that didn't make me feel any better. I preferred to spend time with Americans of European background, and happily, most of our new friends were.

Another chance encounter opened up a world that enchanted me and helped me develop an entirely new way of understanding the art of cooking. I met a Japanese artist, Arakawa, and his wife, the American poet Madeline Gins. Arakawa loved good food and believed that my cooking, which mixed Asian and French ingredients, was fantastic. He thought I should also get to know Japanese cuisine. He talked about dishes I had never heard of like *soba,* a buckwheat noodle that you eat cold, or *shabu shabu,* a dish of thin slices of meat that you twirl in a hot broth. I made him a French potee, a dish of poached meats and vegetables that is served with an aioli sauce; and while you eat, you also sip the rich, golden broth. The dish resonated with Arakawa, as it had the same basic idea as his beloved Japanese dish. He loved it and promised then and there to introduce us to a real Japanese dinner.

One night, he invited us to a Japanese restaurant on Fifty-seventh Street, located at the corner of Park Avenue. I don't remember its name, but I will never forget the meal. I had walked along Central Park on my way to meet them at the restaurant; I had a feeling of well-being. It was an early autumn evening; the sky was clear, and a crisp breeze rustled the red and gold leaves. I felt alive and happy. When I arrived at the restaurant, I was ushered to a beautiful private room whose floor was covered with tatami mats. We sat upon silk pillows on the floor around a lacquered table. In a corner was a tall, black vase that held one apple tree branch with tiny pink flowers. The first course was a soup served in miniature tea pots. The tea pot lid held a little cup, and in the cup was a thin slice of lime. I was told by my host to squeeze the lime into the soup, drink the broth, and then eat the morsels from the little teapot. The broth was clear and warm with a faint taste of fish and flavored with a mushroom that I learned later was the famous Japanese matsutake mushroom, and the zest of the lime came from a citron called Yuzu whose perfume made me swoon. In a single moment, I was warmed by the delicate broth, enthralled by the tastes and textures of what I discovered in my little teapot: a shrimp, two gingko nuts, and several bits of mushroom.

Absorbed in the ritual of the dish, I realized suddenly that this extraordinary soup echoed and prolonged the feeling of calm energy inspired by my autumn walk to the restaurant. The remaining dishes were as extraordinary an experience as the first one: a golden broiled fish, sweet, spicy, swimming in a transparent broth topped with shaved white radish and seaweed, tingling like the autumn breeze. Sake was served in delicate china cups, and at the end of the meal, we were brought warm, smoky tea. For dessert, we were presented with grapes peeled and threaded onto a beautiful carved wooden skewer, with overlapping slices of bright orange persimmons.

I fell in love with Japanese cuisine. Like a visionary dream, the experience of this meal opened up a new world to me. I quickly realized that this was how I wanted to cook. I knew then that I hoped to create a cuisine that would stir emotions in my guests, respond to seasons, and tighten bonds between friends sharing this experience. I realized the importance of the actual container in which the food would be served. I roamed the city looking for beautiful, unusual porcelain from China, Japan, France, and Italy or the best American pieces. I searched New York for Japanese ingredients (they were difficult to find but Arakawa helped), for French and American miniature vegetables, for Chinese mushrooms, for spices, and for fresh fish. I strove to bring elements of surprise and mystery to the table. I decorated my table with branches from our garden, and I garnished dishes with fresh flowers. My friends, astonished by my dinners, begged to be invited, and so once a week, Jimmy and I gathered our friends and our children together for a meal where most of the recipes came out of my imagination.

A year after Marianne was born and as the new fall semester started, I found out that I was pregnant again. Jimmy felt ambivalent about having another child. He thought it was too soon. But I was elated. When I announced to my mother-in-law that the new baby would be born in May, she was very upset, and within a few weeks sent us a television. I guessed, with an inner smirk, that she thought the television would distract us from more amorous activities. I told the Mother Superior that I would give birth in May, and her reaction took me by surprise. I was called to her office. Her face was set in a grim expression, and her mouth was pinched into a straight line. I wondered if one of the student's parents had complained about my teaching.

"Sit down. Mother Elisabeth told me you are expecting another child," she snapped.

"Yes, for the end of May. But don't worry . . . I have someone who will replace me for two months. She is excellent," I assured her.

"We cannot renew your contract," she countered, her bonnet shaking furiously. "You are a good teacher, but we believe that mothers should take care of their children," she continued in a more compassionate tone. "Your child needs you, so we've decided that this is your last year with us. We hope that when your daughter is old enough to go to school, you will consider the convent. We could make some financial arrangement."

"But this is not fair!" I objected, forgetting the intractable nature of the Mother Superior. "Marianne is fine. I have an excellent babysitter." I was crushed. Didn't the church teach that marriage centered around procreation? How could they do this to me? Here I was pregnant again and losing a job that I loved. "But the church says . . ." I attempted.

"Don't bring the church teaching to me!" Mother Superior roared. "The role of a mother is to stay with her children. You *must* give these children you teach a good example. Now go back to your class." It was obvious to me that she wouldn't budge.

What were we going to do? We needed the money, and I wasn't sure I could get another job so easily. Back home that night, I tearfully told Jimmy what had happened. Jimmy told me not to worry, that another job would come along soon. He was now making more money since he had become one of the senior designers in his office, and we could live on his salary alone. He patted my arm, kissed me, and said, "When do we eat?"

➤◄

MUSHROOM FLAN

Clean and remove the stems of 1½ pounds of crimini mushrooms. Puree the mushrooms in a blender with 4 large eggs, salt and pepper, a pinch of nutmeg, 1½ teaspoons of fresh marjoram, and ½ cup of heavy cream. Process until all the ingredients are pureed. Butter 4 small individual soufflé dishes. Fill with the mushroom mixture. Bake in a bain-marie, in a preheated 350° oven for 30 minutes or until the top is golden brown and firm.

Serves 4.

FENNEL SOUP WITH CILANTRO

Thinly slice 3 fresh fennels. In a large saucepan heat 1 tablespoon of butter. Add 1 onion, thinly sliced, and sauté until transparent. Then add 2½ quarts of chicken stock. Add the fennel, and 2 large potatoes, peeled and cubed. Bring to a boil, lower the heat, and cook until the potatoes are done. Puree the soup. Pour the soup back into the saucepan, add salt and pepper to taste, and heat through. Pour the soup in 6 individual bowls. Add 1 tablespoon of crème fraîche to each bowl and sprinkle with 1 tablespoon of chopped cilantro.

Serves 4 to 6.

CHINESE MUSHROOM CONSOMMÉ

This is a very simple recipe made with dry shiitake mushrooms.

Remove the stems of 8 large Chinese dried shiitake mushrooms. Place mushrooms in a bowl and cover with 6 cups of hot water. Soak for 2 hours. Remove the mushrooms and thinly slice. Place mushrooms in a saucepan along with the mushroom water and ½ cup of chicken bouillon. Add salt and pepper to taste. Bring to a boil, lower the heat, and simmer for 10 minutes. Pour the soup with mushrooms in 6 bowls, add 1 small spinach leaf to each bowl, and serve.

Serves 6.

ROAST PORK ON A BED OF POTATOES

Peel 3 garlic cloves and cut in thin slivers. With the point of a knife, make several holes in a 4-pound pork roast to insert the garlic. Rub the pork with 2 tablespoons of soy sauce mixed with ½ tablespoon of sesame oil. Sprinkle the pork with coarse salt and freshly ground pepper. Peel and thinly slice 5 large potatoes. Oil the bottom of a baking pan. Cover the bottom of the pan with the potatoes. Sprinkle with salt and pepper and 2 tablespoons of rosemary. Place the roast pork on top. Add 1 cup of chicken bouillon to the pan and bake in a 350° oven for 1 hour. Add more bouillon if necessary. Remove from the oven and cool for 10 minutes before slicing. Serve with the potatoes.

APPLE MOUSSE

Peel 4 Granny Smith apples. Quarter and remove the center core. Cut the apples in 1-inch pieces. In a skillet, melt 3 tablespoons of butter. Add the apples and cook over low heat until the apples are soft. Remove from the heat. Place the apples in a food processor with ½ cup of sugar and a 2-inch piece of fresh ginger and process until all the ingredients are pureed and let cool. Meanwhile, in a bowl beat 1 cup of heavy cream until stiff. Fold the cream into the apple mixture. Spoon the mousse into 4 wine glasses. Garnish with fresh mint and refrigerate until ready to serve.

Serves 4.

The busy kitchen of our house on Sullivan Street

4

Soho

$\gg\ll$

Juliette was born on June 2, 1959. "Another girl!" Jimmy
muttered when he saw her, "but so beautiful," and he was right.
Juliette was the most beautiful newborn baby I had ever seen. We
sent pictures of the two girls home to Paris. In response, Mira,
my stepfather, sent us tickets to come to Paris to spend the summer with them.

A few days after Juliette was born, Suzanne Chen, my doctor
friend, came to visit and see the new baby.

"Lovely baby, but I have to talk to you both."

"Juliette," she said, "has an eye problem. She has what we call
nystagmus. Her eyes roam without focusing. I don't know how
much she can or will see. It could be temporary but I am not

sure. I want to send you to a friend with whom I studied. He is a great specialist."

We were crushed, worried to death. Was she blind? Would she ever see? What was nystagmus? The next few days were difficult. Suzanne made all the appointments. The end result was that Juliette indeed had nystagmus, a defect of the optic nerve. She would eventually see, but no one could tell us if the problem was temporary or permanent.

It was with a heavy heart that a month later we left for Paris. The summer went quickly. Marianne was learning French words; Juliette, despite her eye problem, was developing into a round, lovely, smiling baby; and my relationship with my mother, for the first time in years, was calm and normal.

In the fall, back in New York, I was looking for a new teaching job. In late September, I was hired to teach French by the Browning School for Boys. To my surprise, on my first day of school, I found out that I was the only woman in a faculty of twenty-seven men! I spent four delightful years there.

In 1960, pregnant once again, we moved to an old house on Nineteenth Street and Cecile, our third daughter, was born on September 15, 1961. Frau Zeimnitz wasn't too happy to look after three children and soon left us. Despite the problems we had finding babysitters, life seemed wonderful. Our children were growing. Juliette could see, and Jimmy was very successful in his work. With my new job, we were financially secure when once again life played a trick on us. I was pregnant again, and this time the school was quite angry with me. They did not think that a pregnant woman should be around growing boys. No law had yet been passed protecting pregnant women from being fired. The school, to my chagrin, let me go.

Thomas was born on November 24, 1965, on Thanksgiving

Day. Three months later, I was hired by Hofstra University to teach French to third-year students.

The place where we were living was now too small for our growing family, so Jimmy and I decided to look for a house. One day a real estate agent I knew called and said that she had a house that she thought I would like. She could not accompany us to see it, so she handed me the key and an address, saying, "Here, take the key and go and see the house. Return the key next week."

That weekend, Jimmy and I went downtown to Sullivan Street below Houston Street to take a look. It was a wide town house, with four stories and an immense garden. I stood in awe of the living room, which was an enormous room with twelve-foot high ceilings and two fireplaces. I could imagine myself sitting in front of a roaring fire reading my favorite novel. For Jimmy, it was a dream: an enormous space with high ceilings and lots of light. We returned several times. I loved the house. I saw the garden's potential and thought that my 4 young children would love it. But the house had no heat and no kitchen, and the rest of the house was a wreck. However, we were determined to buy it. "Don't worry," Jimmy said. "Toothless and I will make it work."

Toothless was the nickname we had given to a jack-of-all-trades we had met a few summers before. For two summers in a row, we had rented an old farmhouse in Hunterdon County, New Jersey for a month. Whenever anything went wrong in the house, which was every other day, we would call our landlord's ex-husband. His name was Bob, but we called him "Toothless" because he didn't have any front teeth. Toothless had served in the merchant marines and was very clever at fixing things without spending a great deal of money. We had become good friends (he adored my cooking), so when in 1967 we moved to a rental house on Nineteenth Street, he agreed to help us fix up the place. He built a kitchen and painted the house with Jimmy. So when Jimmy called him with a promise of a steady job for a few months, plus my cooking, he agreed to come and help rebuild the new house, which we had finally bought after months of negotiation.

I was now very busy packing, I needed good live-in help. This is when Gladys came into our lives. Gladys came from the South. She was a young, plump woman, about twenty-eight years old, and full of joy and laughter. My children loved her, especially Marianne. Gladys would spend hours combing her hair and telling her stories about her boyfriends. I was content that my children were happy and that I had time now to explore our new neighborhood.

Sullivan Street, our part of Sullivan Street that is, began at Houston Street and went all the way to Broome Street. Houston Street is a large avenue that starts at the East River and crosses Manhattan up to the Avenue of the Americas, just below Bleecker Street to the end at the West Side highway. Houston Street divided the neighborhood in two. South of Houston was the Italian working class, and north of Houston was where established urban professionals lived—in the MacDougal/Sullivan Gardens concealed behind rows of 1920s Federal-style town houses.

Our street, along with Thompson Street and West Broadway, was part of an Italian enclave that included a block and a half of MacDougal Street. My intimacy with the neighborhood began even as lawyers were preparing the closing of our house. I walked down Sullivan Street and Thompson Street, looking at the few stores that existed and observing my soon-to-be neighbors. The street was all Italian and mostly elderly. The younger generations had long ago moved to Brooklyn, or Queens, or the outer suburbs. There were also a few Portuguese families living in two or three buildings near Thompson Street. On Sullivan Street, between Houston and Prince, was a *latticini*, Italian for a milk and cheese store. The aroma of freshly made mozzarella and smoked mozzarella wafted through the street. As a new arrival and with the idea that I should become known to the people on the street, every night I would bring a fresh mozzarella home for our dinner. Joe, the owner, also sold and grated Parmesan cheese, olive oil, olives, ricotta, and a few staples. Next door to Joe's was a candy store usually filled with Italian teenagers chatting, or sipping sodas, or doing nothing; at least this is how it seemed to me. Bruno's Bakery was next door. The bakery sold every Italian pastry I had tasted in Italy, plus Italian bread and crackers. Opposite the bakery was the enormous, yet undistinguished front of the parish Church of St. Anthony. The church, run by the Franciscan Friars, had a gray granite façade done in a style that Jimmy called Italianate Grotesque.

On Sundays, Jimmy and I would enjoy a slow walk down Sullivan Street to take in the scene. The church was filled with couples in their best Sunday clothes. Women in long, black, silk dresses, with old-fashioned hats perched on their teased hair. The younger women were more stylish and wore bright colored dresses. No women were wearing slacks. After mass, the women gathered in groups of two or three outside the church, chatting while their husbands in shiny electric blue or pale gray suits stood on the other side of the street in groups in front of Bruno's Bakery. They all carried boxes of pastries. I imagined that the boxes were filled with cannoli, stuffed with a thick sweet cream or babas soaked in rum, for their Sunday meal.

On the corner of Sullivan and Prince streets, this pattern was repeated, but this time by only men who were Portuguese. The rest of the week the St. Anthony Church was closed, except for Bingo Night on Thursday, which took place in the church's basement. Near the church were a group of small stores, one selling homemade sausages, another dealing in haberdashery. An uninviting café with tables, chairs, and a bar was also nearby. Eventually, I would learn that what I took to be a café was actually a social club called the Saxon Knights.

Toward the corner at Prince Street was a butcher shop. What was extraordinary about this butcher shop was that the butcher was a woman. Catherine Carnevari was big, tall, and very strong. I often saw Catherine carrying in a whole side of beef as if it were a bouquet of roses. The store was large with white tiles covering the walls and floor. There were always three or four older women sitting on chairs near a table covered with newspapers, chatting about the neighborhood, their kids, or the latest love triangle. After we moved, I soon joined the women and sat on a chair listening to their chatter. I learned that Catherine was married to a sanitation man half her size, that he was afraid of her, and that she, they whispered when she was not listening, beat him quite often, especially when he came home drunk. Five years later, he died under mysterious circumstances. The whole neighborhood went to the funeral, including myself. Catherine looked even larger dressed all in black. Later that year, to the chagrin of all the women in the neighborhood, Catherine sold the store to a French man who turned it into a pastry shop and café.

At the corner of Prince and Sullivan Streets was a large luncheonette, Vinnie's Coffee Shop. The luncheonette was run by Vinnie and Maria, his mother, who did all the cooking. The white Formica tables were turning dirty yellow with age. At lunch, Vinnie's was full of men and women from the surrounding blocks eating Maria's famous meatball sandwich drowned in her spicy tomato sauce or spaghetti marinara along with cold beer.

In front of our house, which was in the middle of the block, stood De Pauli's grocery store. Just before we moved in, I started to go to De Pauli's to buy sandwiches for our lunch when Vinnie's was too crowded. I loved the store, which had been founded by

Willy De Pauli's grandfather at the turn of the century. Willy was a tall, thin, slightly balding man with a mournful expression on his face. He never really smiled, but he was the nicest man in my new neighborhood. The store was generous, fitted with wood-paneled walls and countless storage cabinets with wood-framed glass doors, filled with hundreds of different types of pasta. Willy sold sandwiches filled with thin slices of mortadella, ham, or cheese on puffy Italian bread. Women would come in, buy a pound of pasta for dinner, and would say to Willy, "I want 5-22-74-5." I wondered what these numbers were. Once we moved in and I felt more secure about my standing with him, I asked Willy what these numbers were for. His answer was, "Not for you. Don't ask! They gamble." And this was all I could get out of him.

Next to De Pauli was Freddie's luncheonette and a Chinese laundry. The laundry was run by a young couple, the Wongs, who had two young children. Thomas, when he was a two-and-half-year-old toddler, befriended them, and I frequently asked them to come and play with him. They often sat on our stoop to play, refusing to come into our house. Tina, the little girl, was beautiful. Thomas, I was sure, had a crush on her. And so for the following three years, until he went to kindergarten, Thomas could be found sitting on our stoop with the other kids, playing with toy cars or stoop ball.

The remaining block was filled with tenements. Then at the corner of Sullivan and Spring streets was an Italian restaurant, the Napoli, run by three sisters. Napoli was the restaurant where you took your Sullivan Street parents for Sunday dinner if you had moved out to the suburbs. The Napoli had a rust-colored stucco façade and illuminated neon beer signs in the window. In front of the restaurant was a narrow bar packed with men with heavy gold chains hanging around their necks, drinking beer, and arguing in loud voices. In the back was a small dining room. By early evening, the restaurant was full. The daily menu was written on a blackboard, and no one asked for the written menu. (I had asked for a menu on my first visit and got a dirty look from the waitress. I never did it again.) You were expected to choose from the blackboard dishes that changed daily. Thursday was my favorite. On that day you could have a plate of tender, succulent tripe in a rich tomato sauce served with lots of hot garlic bread to mop up the sauce. The chicken was also good and so were the mussels on Fridays. My favorite vegetable was the sautéed escarole with thick slices of tender garlic.

Thompson Street, around the corner, was very different. The street had very few stores. There was a Portuguese deli at the corner of Thompson and Prince Streets, a sausage store in the middle of the block, then at the corner of Thompson and Spring Streets was a shop front called The Village Community Problem Center. The people who ran it were trying to help the old Italian families who had battles with their landlords or young mothers whose children had problems either with the police or with school.

But the great attraction of Thompson Street was Mary Finelli's candy store. Mary was born and raised on Thompson Street. At four o'clock after school, her store would be filled with screaming children buying candies for a few pennies. Mary controlled the shouting with a tough teacher's voice and had strict rules. You were not allowed to buy more than two candies. The children often tried going out of the store and coming back in to ask to buy two more. Mary was never fooled, and the children adored her.

In the middle of the block on Prince Street between Thompson Street and West Broadway was the Vesuvio Bakery, run by a small man with slicked down black hair called Tony Dapolito. He looked like an Italian lover from movies of the 1930s. I was told by the real estate agent who had sold us the house that Tony Dapolito was the defacto Mayor of South Village, but his real power base was the territory between West Broadway and Sixth Avenue. Tony sold several different breads and crunchy bread-sticks. The best ones were hard dried toasts called pizzelli, which were used for dipping in soup or for absorbing hot Italian tomato sauce. I first experienced them at Napoli, where they were served with mussels marinara on Fridays. I wanted to be in Tony Dapolito's good graces, so every afternoon on my way back from work, I bought these sublime toasts either peppered or plain, or some golden, crunchy bread sticks to take with me to work the next day.

It was impossible for a young, struggling couple like Jimmy and I to carry a mortgage on the new house while paying for the rental on Nineteenth Street, not to mention paying Toothless and buying materials to redo the new house. So we decided to move into our Sullivan Street house immediately. I started to pack our household possessions. Naima and Toothless helped. I packed our clothes in large wardrobe boxes, and everyone, including the movers, laughed at me as I wrote "close" on each box. We moved into an empty house that had only a single toilet and one wash basin on the first floor. There was no kitchen, no bathroom. The radiators barely got warm from a frail steam-heating system whose boiler was in the next door neighbor's house, the Brods, who had bought their house at the same time as we bought ours. Naturally, they wanted us to get a new heating system immediately. This was going to be expensive, but it had to be done. Therefore, our first priority was to find a real plumber. I also had other worries.

"How do we live in this empty house with four children, the youngest only 18 months old?" I asked Jimmy. "I don't think we can do it!"

"Yes we can. We'll put our bed in the living room and place the children's mattresses on the floor next to us. We will buy a microwave oven to heat breakfast, an electric kettle for tea, paper plates and cups, and for dinner, we will go out and explore all the local restaurants. No problem; you will see."

I took two weeks off from Hofstra University to pack and organize the move. Within two days, we had moved, and then the problems really started.

Thomas was crawling all over the place. The floor was not the best place for him. Toothless had removed the linoleum that was covering the stairway, exposing the nails. While he removed the nails on the three flights of stairs, we had to watch Thomas like hawks. Gladys could do little else but keep an eye on him. Then we had to teach him how to go down the steps, getting him to sit on the first step, then slide down on his bottom, just in case he escaped us. Finally, he succeeded, and with great peals of laughter, he reached the lowest floor.

The next problem was washing ourselves and our four children. The three girls went to school every day and could not look like dirty urchins. How do you wash kids with no hot water, no shower, and no bathroom?

I made a list of all our friends who lived within a ten-block radius and begged. Could we impose on them, once a week, all six of us to come and take showers? I was delighted by their responses. They all came to the rescue. So on Mondays, we bathed at Elisabeth Fonseca's house; on Tuesdays we bathed at the Ghents; Wednesdays were bad because no one could have us; but on Thursdays and Fridays, we went to our neighbor, Mrs. Brod's, apartment, and on the weekends, to my in-laws. After one month, I was afraid that I had used all my friends' good will and started to apologize profusely. They all told me not to worry. Soon, we found a plumber who promised that within a month the top floor bathroom would be finished.

Having established a routine for the children and us, after my two weeks' leave, I was ready to go back to teaching. The morning I was to return to work, I got up very quietly. Since we were all sleeping in one room, I decided I would have a coffee across the street at Freddie's luncheonette.

As I entered, I looked around. I was astonished by the crowd at the counter. I was the only woman in the place; most of the men looked as if they were construction workers, and there were two policemen in uniform. They were all drinking beer or hard liquor and wine. Freddie's was a bar, not a luncheonette! Freddie, I assumed it was Freddie himself behind the bar, was short, plump, with very thick glasses. He looked at me and said in a very polite, but gruff voice, "What you want?"

"Could I have a cup of coffee and an English muffin?"

"I haven't served a cup of coffee in twenty years! Who are you? Where do you live?"

"Across the street, 114, in the big house."

Suddenly, one of the men drinking called to me: "Have a drink . . . on me . . . come on beautiful, have a drink."

I was about to leave when Freddie took my side and said: "Leave the lady alone."

All the men suddenly kept quiet and looked sheepishly at Freddie.

"Today, I can't give you any coffee, lady, but tell me what you want every day and at what time. It will be here for you."

"I go to work Monday, Wednesday, and Friday. Could I have coffee and an English muffin?"

"You got it!" Freddie said with a grimace that was a smile.

And so three times a week, at six o'clock in the morning, my coffee and English muffin would be waiting for me. The men at the counter now greeted me with a warm "Hi." Freddie never allowed them to be rude or familiar with me.

A few days later, wanting to thank him for his kindness, I entered his luncheonette in the early afternoon. To my surprise, the scene had radically changed. The counter was packed with women drinking soda or juices. Freddie's wife, Marie, was now behind the counter chatting with the women. The opposite of Freddie, Marie was a tall, plump woman with grayish hair and a sweet smile. Every afternoon, just before school let out, the women would gather in the luncheonette while Marie would hold court, giving advice on numerous subjects from a pasta recipe to what to do when your daughter was dating someone you did not like because he was not Italian. Some of the women, I also learned, were widows or older women whose husbands were playing "Bocci," the Italian ball game in special bars on MacDougal Street or sipping espresso at their social club. The luncheonette was a sort of social club for the women who had nowhere else to go. Marie had two children, a son and a daughter. The daughter was married and lived across the street from the luncheonette. Their son, Andy, was a problem, I had heard from sitting in the butcher store. He took drugs and was often drunk. Often, one could see him walking down Sullivan Street, muttering to himself while the old ladies would shake their heads in disgust. Years later, when both Marie and Freddie died and the luncheonette was sold to become a beauty salon, the old ladies lost their meeting place. Some died; others left the street to join their children in Queens, and a few elected the beauty salon as their new meeting place because the salon was run by a beautiful, young Italian woman, Pat, who knew everyone on the street. Years later, Pat and I became good friends, and when she decided to move her beauty salon two doors down, Jimmy designed it for her.

In the first months of living in the house, we had solved the problem of feeding the family. On Monday, Wednesday, and Friday I sent all four children to Luigi's Restaurant at the corner of Prince and Sullivan streets, where Luigi's wife would take care of them. The restaurant was a dark long room with banquettes on both sides. In front there was a bar, and around 5:00 P.M., it was always filled with workers having a drink before heading home. Most nights the children ate pasta, meatballs, and salad. Jimmy and I ate sandwiches in the living room. The other two days and on weekends, I cooked in the fireplace. I used a hibachi, a small Japanese barbeque set in the hearth. In fact, I became quite an expert on cooking in the fireplace. We had lived in Italy, in Umbria, where cooking in the fireplace was common place. For example, veal chops were marinated in a mixture of lemon juice, olive oil, and herbs for a couple of hours, then grilled over hot coals. I also learned what vegetables would cook easily and quickly. Eggplant, thinly sliced and brushed with olive oil, cooked in a few minutes as did fresh shiitake or portobello mushrooms. Grated carrots tossed with lemony vinaigrette made a delicious salad, and frozen, tiny green peas could be heated in the microwave. That month, we ate a lot of hamburgers, pork chops, and veal chops.

Slowly, the house started to take shape. On weekends, Jimmy and I both worked side by side with Toothless. I painted the children's bathroom, learned how to tape plasterboard, and removed linoleum with a blow torch. The children's room was finally finished, and they all moved to the top floor.

One Saturday, I sanded the front door and painted it with glossy black paint. To my horror, the next morning the front door was all scratched and my work was destroyed. I was very upset and decided to repaint it and try to catch who had done it. But since I could not work until the following weekend, I had to wait. Jimmy and I now slept alone in the living room. One night, unable to sleep, still quite upset by the front door incident, I got up and walked toward the window, looking at the street, silent and empty. Suddenly I saw a young boy running toward our house, a rag in his hand. He climbed the stoop, lit the rag with a match, and was about to run down when, in an instant, I was outside in my nightgown and grabbed him by the hair. I pushed away the furiously burning rag soaked with gasoline and started screaming, shaking him like a leaf.

"Who are you? What's your name? Who sent you? Answer. . . . I'll call the police . . ."

A few minutes later, I found myself surrounded by about ten women. Still holding the boy by the hair, I screamed, "Who's your mother? Where is she? Where do you live? What's your name? Answer or I will call the police."

The boy slowly pointed to one of the women standing by.

I dragged the child in front of her.

"Is he yours?"

She whispered, "Yes."

For a second, I did not know what to do. *Should I call the police?* I was still in my nightgown, so I made a quick decision.

"Take him home. If I see him within ten feet from my house, I will file a complaint. Now tell me where you live?"

"Two houses down," she answered, taking the boy by the arm. "Don't worry; it won't happen again."

The next morning I told Toothless what had happened. He sat me down and said, "Let me tell you about the street. This is Mafia territory. You have invaded their turf, and they don't know who you are. They are very good people, family people; they just don't want someone not Italian living here."

As I was about to protest that we were also a hardworking family, he shook his head and continued: "Freddie, who is so nice to you, collects the money for the number games. Do you see the black limousine on Friday nights parked in the street? They come to collect it. Willie takes down the numbers, collects the money, and gives it to Freddie. You know the social club down the street?

This is where they gather and discuss their affairs. You are intruding. Give them time. The best thing you did was not to call the police."

The next day on my way home from work, I stopped at the social club and sat down at one of the empty tables. A few men were playing cards; they looked baffled to see me there. A fat, middle age man stood up and walked toward me. *He must be the owner,* I thought, and so I asked him for a coffee.

"We don't serve coffee."

"A glass of juice, any kind of juice?"

"No juice! We serve nothing."

This was clearly not Freddie's Luncheonette. No one here was going to acknowledge my presence, let alone accommodate me. The man walked away, and so I sat there silently; then I started to talk.

"I am the new owner of 114. . . . I am French, and we have four children. . . . I work as a teacher, and my husband is an architect . . ."

No answer, no sign that anyone was listening.

"I work hard, so does he. We are not rich. . . . I chose this neighborhood because I had an Italian *ballia* (wet nurse). . . . My first words were Italian." Still no reaction. "And I love our house. We feel so safe . . . like in a village. I want my children to grow up here."

As I got no reaction, I stood up and left, saddened.

That night I told Jimmy what I did and how I had failed.

"Don't worry. You know what Toothless said; they will get used to us."

For the next few weeks, nothing happened. Our bedroom was finished, so we moved to our floor. Now we had two bathrooms and no need to bother our friends. The next task was to create a kitchen out of the former outhouse. Toothless had found an old Italian tile setter in the neighborhood, and so Jimmy ordered a ton of sand for the dining room and kitchen.

A few days later, at 7:00 A.M., the front door bell rang. I ran to open the door and faced a man holding papers.

"Rossant? I have your sand. Please sign here."

Once I signed, I saw the truck turn around and dump one ton of sand on the sidewalk.

"But you can't do that. It has to be in bags! How will we bring it in?"

"Lady, this is not my problem, but a word of advice—if you don't want a ticket start bringing it in right away."

I woke up Jimmy, the three girls, and Gladys and told them to take pots and pans, and together we would bring in the sand through the basement door.

We must have been a sight! The three little girls in their pajamas, Thomas jumping on the sand, me in my dressing gown, Gladys in a short nightie, and Jimmy, the only one half-dressed. We formed a line. I filled the pots, Jimmy at the other end emptied them; in between, the others passed the pots and pans.

Within ten minutes, we were surrounded by muscled young men from the neighborhood lugging enormous containers, and in a half hour, the sand was in the house. I made coffee for everyone, realizing that my speech at the social club had worked. We were now part of the street scene and accepted by the neighborhood.

One morning in June, after we had been in the house six months, I saw that the street was crossed by high-illuminated arches every ten feet. I asked Willy what they were for.

"Don't you know? It is for St. Anthony's Fair. It lasts two weeks, with stands selling sausages, zeppole, and pizza, and there is gambling and games like throwing baseballs or catching small fish. Officially, the fair is run by the church, but really it's run by Mike. You will see him around collecting the fees for the church. You can't miss him; he is always screaming at everybody. Then on the last day of the fair, there is a procession with a statue of the Virgin paraded up and down the street, her dress pinned with dollar bills. There is lots of music and a live band. You will love it!"

A few days later, we saw a truck pulling an immense stand and stopping in front of our house. The first one to set up his stand in front of our house was a man who sold sausages, sweetbreads, and beer. Although he would appear with the fair for the next thirty years, I never learned his name, but he was by far the most popular vendor in the fair. Short, skinny, and adorned with a swooping white mustache, a white chef's hat perched on his bald head, a red handkerchief around his neck, all day long and all night til two in the morning, he called people to his stand, through a loudspeaker, making jokes and telling the crowds how wonderful his sausages were. Every morning his assistant, a fat, older man, sat on a chair near our house peeling a mountain of onions while the sausage man prepared his sweet breads and sausages. The street was full of stinking garbage. No one seemed to sweep, and by the second day, I was incensed. After work, I went to him to complain about the garbage all over the street and our stoop. He offered me a sausage sandwich. I was going to refuse, but the sausage sandwich looked tempting, so I accepted. I bit into the hot sweet sausage with great pleasure. I had to admit that it was excellent. I smiled and asked again if, at the end of the day, he could sweep all around his stand and my stoop? He promised he would do his best. But at the end of the first weekend, the garbage was worse; people sat on our stoop eating, dropping greasy onions on the steps. I hosed it down every morning, cursing the fair and everyone around. One day I decided to put sawdust on the steps, hoping that people would not sit on the stoop. I was wrong. Nothing could stop them from sitting there. I called St. Anthony's Church and spoke to the Father in charge of the fair. Father R. promised to help. However, after two days, the garbage was overflowing and despite my begging the stands in front of our house to sweep every night, the garbage kept on accumulating.

A week after the fair was over, I went around the private houses on Sullivan and MacDougal streets and invited the owners to come and discuss the fair over a drink in our empty living room. I asked Father R. to also join us. My guests that night were Herbert Ferber, the sculptor, and his wife, Edith, with whom we would become very good friends; the Brods, a young real estate man who, with his wife, had bought the house at the corner of Prince; and finally a couple who lived further down on Sullivan Street. Everyone accepted and came. We talked about the fair, the garbage, and the loud music. Father R. promised that the fair would be cleaner the following year. He would ask the Sanitation Department for more garbage cans, and he would see that each stand swept around itself. But I wanted more. I wanted the fair to move somewhere else.

A few days later as I entered our local liquor store, the owner, Andrew, a middle-age man who, Willy told me, still lived with his mother and swept the church's steps every morning before attending mass, asked me to follow him to a small room behind the counter. He offered me a chair, and he stood over me.

"You have to stop trying to move the fair or making trouble. You will be hurt. People here love the fair. It has been here for fifty years. Who are you, and who gives you the right to make trouble?"

I sat there speechless. I loved the street, and I could not fathom that the other people living on the street liked the fair. I looked up at Andrew. He was looking at me seriously, not smiling. I got up and left without a word.

Upset and worried, I went home and decided not to tell Jimmy about the lecture. The next morning I saw a letter stuck in the front door. It was written in bad English, and the gist of it was: If I continued trying to move the fair, they would break my legs and set the house on fire. I will never know who *they* were. It could have been Andrew or some other people from the social club down the street. The warning was strong enough for me to cease and desist. I would have to live with the fair.

The following year, our children decided to have a stand in front of the house and serve French crêpes with sugar or jam. Jimmy built them a small stand. I got a small electric hot plate and pan and made the batter. Marianne, Juliette, and Cecile spent the weekend making crêpes. They were so successful selling crêpes that Mike came around and told me I had to pay for the right to have a stand. I was incensed. I called Father R. and said that I refused to pay for using my own sidewalk! We finally agreed that I would not pay Mike, but I would make a donation to the church. The following weekend, Calvin Trillin, our friend, passing by the fair, saw my three adorable little girls selling crêpes. He did not realize that they were our children, and the following week, he had a story about them in *The New Yorker*.

As the years went by, I started to like the fair. It was like a small village fair filled with children screaming up and down the street, eating candy, and playing games. On the weekend, I gave our children some money to eat and play at the fair. Sometimes after work, I would walk through the fair and could not resist picking up a couple of zeppole, the round, fried dough rolled in sugar. They were hot, greasy, crunchy, and delicious. On weekends, I would invite friends for dinner and order zeppole from a fat lady at the corner of Sullivan and Spring streets to serve my guests as dessert. Yes, I was softening, but I still hated the fair's garbage. I continued fighting with the Church for thirty years. The year we sold our house, the church, realizing that the street had changed and that the Italians had moved out to be replaced with more upscale people, decided to eliminate the fair! I was astonished and somewhat sad and nostalgic. One more tradition that had made Sullivan Street so wonderful, disappearing just as we were moving out!

When the house was finally finished, we decided to give a big party to celebrate. We did not have furniture or any money to buy some. So Jimmy had a brilliant idea: cover the windows and the round ornate plaster rosaces on the ceiling with Christmas lights and leave the place empty like the ballroom it resembled. We hired a three-piece Greek band and sent some 300 invitations. For the invitations, he made a picture showing the front of the whole house opening with the empty rooms of the house behind. Was it because of Jimmy's drawing or because people were curious about the house, that every one said yes? Jimmy was worried: Would the living room floor hold so many people dancing?

I had another worry: What to serve three-hundred people? I went to see Catherine, the butcher, for advice. She suggested serving *cotechino,* a large fat sausage, with lentils. She would make me about twenty cotechinos. "You can cook them in advance, slice them when cold, and heat them the night of the party in the oven. Very easy." Jimmy and I were still faced with the problem of what else to serve. We had very little money and so many guests!

"I know," Jimmy said, "let's go to the Bronx Terminal market two days before the party."

We got up a five in the morning and drove to the terminal market, which was located near the Yankee Stadium. The market was clogged with enormous trucks loading and unloading. We parked and walked around. I saw cases of sweet peppers, red, orange and green. So we bought a case to make a tri-color salad in lemony vinaigrette. Further down, we found a case of endive to glaze with sugar. Then I saw crates of tangerines and thought that they would make a great dessert by placing the tangerines in a large bowl in the center of the table. With our shopping done, it was now 7:30 A.M., and we were famished. We stopped at a diner. It was packed with workers from South America eating eggs, sausages, rice, and beans. We ordered the same with a strong black Cuban coffee and had the best breakfast ever.

One day before the party, I also made Cairo-style *babaghanou* and *tarama* salad. I planned to place four different types of olives everywhere and thin slices of Italian salamis and mozzarella from Joe's store. I also made an enormous green salad. Catherine had suggested that I serve tiny cannoli and that she would talk to Bruno, the owner of the bakery down the street. She was sure he would give me a special price. I rented a few chairs for older people, dishes, forks, knives, plates, napkins, and a table for the wine and soda. I found an unemployed actor who agreed to serve the drinks.

Jimmy had decided that I should wear a Greek outfit, so we had gone shopping in a Greek store, near Third Avenue and Fifty-ninth Street. We chose a long dress in off-white cotton with lace around the waist. Jimmy also bought me a necklace and long earrings. A few days in advance of the party, I told the neighborhood that we were having a very large party to celebrate the end of the construction. Willy spread the word, and on the night of the party, there were no cars parked on the street so that guests could park easily. For the first hour, no one came, and I got very nervous. The bartender tried to calm me down. "You are in Manhattan," he said with a little smile. "People feel they have to be fashionably late." And as the Greek band played with gusto, I, in my Greek long dress, stood waiting, thinking no one will come down to this neighborhood!

Was I wrong! They arrived, it seemed to me, all at once. I greeted people, some I did not even know. We danced, and at 10:00 P.M., I called people over to eat. And they ate and ate, as Jimmy and I, still worrying about the floor, refilled the platters.

We danced again, chatted, drank, and had a great time. The party ended at three o'clock in the morning. No one on the street complained. Years later, I would meet people whom I did not know who would insist they knew us. "I was at a party at your house years ago. It was great, and the food was fantastic!"

➤◄

MUSSELS WITH HOT TOMATO SAUCE

Wash and clean 4 pints of mussels. Set aside. In a heavy saucepan, heat 2 tablespoons of olive oil. Add ½ cup of chopped parsley; 1 medium onion, finely chopped; 1 small carrot, scraped and finely chopped. Cook, stirring for 5 minutes, then add 3 garlic cloves, finely chopped, along with 1 cup of chopped fresh basil. Mix well and cook for 4 minutes. Then add a 14-ounce can of whole tomatoes with the juice, a pinch of salt, and ½ teaspoon of hot pepper flakes. Bring to a boil, lower the heat, and simmer for 40 minutes or until the sauce has thickened. Set aside.

In a large saucepan, melt 2 tablespoons of butter. When the butter is hot, add 2 garlic cloves, minced, along with 5 tablespoons of chopped parsley. Cook for 2 minutes, then add the mussels, mix well, cover, and cook over medium heat for 10 minutes or until the mussels are all open. Then pour in the tomato sauce, mix well, and serve with thick slices of warm Italian bread.

Serves 4.

BROILED VEAL CHOPS

Place 4 1-inch thick veal chops in a pan. In a bowl, mix together the juice of 1 lemon with 4 tablespoons of olive oil, salt and pepper, 1 tablespoon of rosemary, 1 tablespoon of thyme, and 1 tablespoon of sage. Mix well. Pour over the veal chops and refrigerate for 1 hour, turning the veal chops several times.

Broil over hot coals for 6 minutes on each side or until the veal chops are golden brown. Serve with steamed corn and a salad.

Serves 4.

CRÊPES WITH SUGAR AND JAM

In a food processor, place ¼ cup of flour with ¾ cup of milk, 3 eggs, 2 tablespoons of melted butter, 1 tablespoon of sugar, and a pinch of salt. Process until all the ingredients are well mixed. Pour the batter in a bowl and let stand for at least 1 hour.

Melt some butter in a rather flat skillet or a crêpe pan. When the butter bubbles, pour 3 tablespoons of batter and quickly tilt and rotate the pan until the batter covers the entire surface. When the edges begin to brown, turn the crêpe with a spatula and cook the other side for a few seconds. Slide the crêpe on a dish. Sprinkle the crêpes with sugar and melted butter or with jam and melted butter.

If you wish to make several crêpes before serving them, cover with wax paper and continue cooking. The crêpes can be kept warm in a 225° oven.

Makes about 16 crêpes.

Teaching children how to cook as part of Art Park, Lewiston, New York

5

Cooking with Colette

A year after Thomas was born, I was hired by Hofstra University to teach French literature to future French teachers. Three times a week, I drove to the Hofstra campus in Long Island early in the morning and came home around four o'clock just as my daughters were returning from school. One morning in January, I woke up to six inches of snow. My car was an old jalopy, and I didn't trust it on the snow and ice. For the first time, I took the train to school. I arrived at the Hempstead station, looking in vain for a taxicab to take me to Hofstra. Next to me stood a young woman wrapped in a fur coat. I asked her if she knew how I could get to the university from the station. I said I was late for my class and quite worried because I was a new teacher and still on trial. The young woman said, "I also teach at Hofstra, in the English department. Let's call for a taxi and share it. Don't worry; everyone will be late today, including the students. By the way, I am Alice Trillin. I also live in Manhattan."

Alice was a beautiful young woman with light wavy blonde hair and large eyes. She talked rapidly and had an easy laugh. I liked her immediately, and very soon, I invited her and her husband to dinner. Calvin, "Bud" to those close to him, was a writer for *The New Yorker*. He was charming, always joking and teasing us. He loved good food, and I loved having a guest who looked forward to my new way of cooking and my experiments.

When we met, Jimmy and I had just moved into our Sullivan Street house, and the Trillins were not far away on Grove Street; a pleasant walk through the village was all that separated us. I loved to have them over for dinner; every time I found some interesting ingredient or a new Chinese restaurant, I would invite them over. Now feeling more secure and bold, I explored many small streets and back alleys in Chinatown. Chinatown was growing very fast, and I was never far behind. I discovered new restaurants and new markets, was not afraid to ask questions, buy ingredients that were strange to me, and try them at home. Sometimes the experiments were great achievements, sometimes even greater disasters. I would call Suzanne and tell her about my disasters, and we both would laugh, then she would explain how the Chinese cooked with whatever ingredients I had been too original with.

A few weeks before Alice and Calvin's first daughter, Abigail, was born, I called Alice: "Alice, I just found a new vegetable in Chinatown. They call it water spinach; it is yummy. Come for dinner tomorrow night."

Come they did, and after we had eaten the appetizer, a cauliflower soup with blue cheese, Alice announced in an excited voice, "I have to go home; I think the baby is coming. Bud, take me home."

Calvin got up and said in a hurt tone, "But I don't know what Colette is serving for the main course!"

We all laughed, and I went to the kitchen and made the dinner "to go." I placed the roasted quails that I was going to serve with the water spinach in a container along with some sautéed water chestnuts and said, as I handed him the package, "Don't worry; first babies take a long time. Here is what I would have served you. Good luck."

Abigail took another week to come, but the story of my care package ended up as a small story in one of Calvin's books. In *Alice Let's Eat,* he wrote, "One of my favorite New York cooks is a friend of ours named Colette Rossant . . . She defies Americanization, and she is so far above frozen food, that I always suspected that she may not keep ice cubes." The book was reviewed everywhere, and *The Wall Street Journal* used this quote to praise Trillin's book. All of a sudden the telephone started to ring, and requests poured in for articles about food. The first call was from *Vogue,* asking me to contribute to a series of articles by well-known cooks about dinners that had not gone as planned. I said yes right away. I certainly had the right material. Only a few weeks before, my husband had asked me to invite one of his clients, a rich developer with whom he was involved in a very large project. Jimmy had talked about me as a wonderful cook, and the man wanted to be invited to dinner.

"You have to go all out," Jimmy said. "It's very important for me."

I planned the menu very carefully. I decided to make a cheese soufflé as a starter (serving a soufflé in 1968 was still exotic, but this is no longer true today), half a young goat as the main course served with Chinese vegetables, and a puree spiced with black olives. For dessert I would make a beet pie. I had never made one, but I thought it should be quite easy. I went shopping on

Ninth Avenue in Asian stores, which I had recently discovered, and bought a baby goat. I cooked all day. The pie was beautiful, the color of ruby; the goat was ready to be put in the oven and the table set. At 7:00 P.M. I put my baby goat, smeared with spices and French mustard, in the oven. The developer, his wife, and two of his associates arrived promptly, and at 8:00 P.M. we all sat down with what I thought would be a memorable evening.

The first course went well. The golden soufflé had not collapsed, and I thought that our guests were quite impressed. Once the plates were cleared, I took the baby goat out of the oven and tried to carve it. Impossible! I called Jimmy, who sharpened our knife and tried also. Still impossible. I had underestimated the cooking time. The goat was underdone and disaster threatened.

"Quickly go and pour more wine and give them fresh bread. Tell them that what I am making has to be done at the last minute and may take some time."

I raised the oven temperature to 450 degrees and waited ten more minutes. Still tough. This was not a baby goat I had bought; this was his grandmother! And so while they all drank more wine, I tore pieces of meat from the goat, cut it into tiny cubes. I wondered what I could make and decided on an omelet. I stuffed it with the goat cubes, lots of herbs, and garlic. I wasn't very sure what it would taste like but hoped that the herbs would enhance the dish. I also hoped that no one would think that the omelet was a very unusual and bizarre dish. To this day, I don't know what Jimmy thought of the dinner. All I know is that, as they left, the guests praised the dinner, raving about my food and the very unusual omelet. Had they been too drunk to notice the taste of goat? The article about the goat was a success, more offers for articles came my way, and thus my career as a food writer was born.

One day when Juliette, our second daughter, was in the fifth grade, she announced that many of her friends had formed secret clubs. She wanted to form a secret club herself but had no ideas. What could she do? I suggested a cooking club. The idea came from the fact that when I came home from work, my children would be all around me clamoring for my attention. I began to give them jobs to do in the kitchen. I taught them how to peel vegetables, stir the sauces, etc. I told Juliette to select a few friends and invite them to our house one Saturday a month to learn how to cook one dish that they would eat for lunch and another they would take home. Juliette would charge a quarter. She was enthusiastic and came back the next day triumphant, saying that she had four new friends who would join us at the end of the week for the first meeting of the secret cooking club.

That first Saturday, I had in my kitchen five little girls eagerly waiting to be taught how to cook. I was scared. It is one thing to show your child how to separate an egg, but now I had children I did not really know who looked at me eagerly and were probably expecting a miracle: In one day, they would know how to cook!

I had decided that each child would make a quiche for lunch and a small apple pie to take home. And so I gave each child a bowl, a wooden spoon, a knife, flour, etc. I went from child to child teaching each how to measure, wiping the spills, and praying that the dough would work. We made the dough that I call "The never-miss dough," the one that my own grandmother had taught me as a little girl in Egypt. I taught the girls how to break eggs and separate the yolks from the whites, allowing the whites to slide in their hands into the bowl. "Disgusting" said one little girl, laughing as the yolk also fell in the bowl, and I picked it up with my hands. We beat the yolks with cream, grated Swiss cheese, rolled the dough, and lined the pie plates with the dough. We beat the whites and folded the beaten whites into the yolks. Soon the quiches were assembled, and the five little girls, trembling with excitement, each placed their quiche in the oven.

While they baked, we made a French open apple pie with the remaining dough. The children were going to take the uncooked apple pies home to bake.

When the quiches were ready, we all sat around the table and ate. For most of the children, this was their first taste of a quiche. "I love it!" cried one the girls. This was followed by grunts of approval from the other children. The day had been a great success. Juliette was happy, and as they left the house, she handed them the recipes of what they had made.

I was exhausted but pleased to see the smile of contentment on my little girl's face. On Monday, when Juliette returned from school, she announced that other girls in the class, having learned how much fun the five friends had had, wanted to join the club. "Can I invite other friends to come?" Juliette asked.

I did not think that I could afford to have so many children. At a quarter per child, I would quickly go broke. Also, more than five would be too much to handle. I said to Juliette, "We will see next month. Maybe the ones who wanted to join now will have forgotten about your secret club. You can invite the same children to come back." But time did nothing to dull their enthusiasm. By the end of April, I had about twenty mothers call me to ask if their children could join the club. "I hear that you really teach them how to cook and that they loved it. I never learned anything from my mother. She never taught me! I am such a bad cook. . . . I really wish you would reconsider and take my daughter."

One night our friend, Alan Buschbaum, came by. Alan was an architect, a graphic designer, and above all, my best friend. What we had in common was cooking as he was one of the best cooks I knew in New York. He and I often cooked together. I told him of my predicament. "What should I do?" I asked.

"I know. Let's make it a *real* cooking school. You will charge for teaching. You can teach every Saturday morning. I will design a flyer, and you can send it to all the private schools. Parents have no idea of what to do with their children on Saturday. You will be a godsend to the mothers."

And true to his word, Allan made a flyer announcing COLETTE'S COOKING SCHOOL. We calculated how much the food and the utensils would cost and decided what to charge the parents. We mailed the flyer to all the private schools. The school would start the first Saturday in June, when private schools began their summer vacation. Alan secretly sent the flyer to Corky Pollen, *New York* Magazine's "Best Bet" editor. She mentioned the cooking school in her column, and we received hundreds of calls. This time it was not only girls who wanted to come but also boys. I decided that we would have three sessions a week. Each session would have eight kids: four boys and four girls. I also had to make some rules. The children had to be at least eight, tall enough to look in a saucepan without going on tiptoe. A few days before the first class, I had a call from *The New York Times*. They had heard about the school and wanted to send a reporter. I tried to dissuade them as they wanted to come on the first day of school. Couldn't they wait? No was the answer. As the parents dropped their children at our house, a reporter roamed among them, asking questions.

We were all in the dinning room. Each child had a wooden chopping board, a small knife, wooden spoons, bowls, etc. For the first session, as I knew I had a reporter looking on, I decided to stick with the same dishes we had made at Juliette's first cooking club meeting. We made eight quiches and eight apple pies. To my relief, the quiche came out of the oven golden brown. The kids loved them, even the little girl who kept on saying, "I hate eggs," relished the quiche.

In one of my Saturday classes was the daughter of a television producer. He came to see my class and suggested that we make a pilot and present it to PBS. PBS loved the idea but refused to put up the money, so he turned to Warren Steibel, a well-known television producer who was also the producer of William Buckley's *Firing Line,* a political talk show filmed in South Carolina.

Warren Steibel decided to present the idea to South Carolina public television, which accepted the sponsorship of the show. As the school year had started by this time and I was back to teaching at Hofstra, we decided that I would start filming the show in July. He flew me to Columbia to start filming. The plan was to do twelve episodes. Four boys and four girls would join me for each episode, and each show would be geared to a different age group, ending with a Christmas dinner aimed at older children.

To get children to join the show, Warren put me on South Carolina public radio, asking children to come to the studio to interview for a cooking show. The response was overwhelming. Hundreds of children swarmed into the radio station. Warren refused to let me see any of the children, saying that the element of surprise as I met them on the set would make for a better television show. We decided together that the first show would be about dough, pies, cracking eggs, etc. The first taping went well; however, Warren had failed to factor in that the children were Southerners with heavy southern drawls, and I had a French accent. The dialogue between the children and I was as funny as an Abbot & Costello sketch. I dimly understood what they were saying, and they barely understood me, but we managed.

Another problem was finding the ingredients for the cooking show. Columbia was not New York. No artichokes, no really fresh vegetables, and the only salad available was iceberg lettuce. For every show, we had to scramble for ingredients. Sometimes they were flown in from New York; other times we appealed to the public.

On one of the shows, we were going to make a watercress

soup. The staff was unable to find any. Watercress, I was told, was not available in Columbia. "Impossible," I said. "Watercress grows everywhere." So I went on the air, asking people who lived in the suburbs of Columbia and who had a brook in their backyard, to look for wild watercress, describing the small green leaves as clearly as possible. The next day, we had a line of cars and trucks filled with watercress arriving at the studio. We made the soup, and the town of Columbia got hooked on it!

For the last show, the average age of the children was fifteen. I decided that I would teach them how to prepare and roast a goose. We had the usual problem: No geese were available in Columbia. Warren decided that he would order them from New York. A day before filming, we received nine geese. I would roast one and place it in the set's oven. The next day each child would prepare one. While we prepared the geese and chatted about Christmas presents and what the children ate for their Christmas dinners, (no one had ever eaten or seen a goose before! They ate ham or turkey.) the aroma of the cooked goose wafted through the studio. When we were finished preparing the geese, I went to the oven and removed the cooked goose. Usually, as I set prepared dishes on the table, Warren would scream "cut," and the children would then grab what they had prepared. This time Warren forgot to say "cut." As I set the goose on the table, everyone in the studio rushed to the table to get a taste of the goose, fighting with the children. All of that went on the tape!

In September, the show was aired on PBS stations around the country, and *The New York Times* television critic loved it and praised it, calling it a "a very funny show, one that children and parents should watch together."

I was now quite busy, teaching at Hofstra, running the cooking school, and writing food articles. One day, Alan called me to invite me to lunch with a friend of his who wanted to meet me.

Barbara Plummer was, I found out midway through the lunch, the senior editor at Scribner's. She asked me to talk about my ideas on a cookbook for children. A cookbook for children? I looked at Alan, who looked the other way. *What had he told her? Was I to talk about a book I hadn't even thought about?* So I invented a book on the spot. Looking up at Barbara, I said, "Yes, I want to write a cookbook for children based on my cooking school. The book would start with desserts and end up with vegetables. I will tell a story about how I learned to cook. The recipes will be simple but real. There will be 'no mud pies!', and I think that Jimmy should illustrate the book with line drawings. Children will love them."

Barbara loved the idea, and a month later I received a contract. I was in a state of panic. *Write a book?* I did not know how and where to begin. I could not type, could not spell, and at that time, there were no computers to help you along. What was I going to do? I called my friend Lorraine Davis. She had been my editor at *Vogue*. Lorraine had assigned me my first story and had remained a staunch supporter. "Very easy," she said. "Buy a tape recorder, sit down, and talk into the microphone. Then give the tapes for someone to type. Read them, correct the recipes, and send me the manuscript. I will edit it. You are a storyteller, so don't worry."

I did not know how I was going to write with the children out of school and needing my constant supervision. It was July, so Elisabeth Fonseca suggested that I send the children to her house in East Hampton, along with Lucy, our new housekeeper. I would come on the weekends and that would allow me time to write all week. Lucy was my gift from the gods. Gladys had stayed with us until the house was finished. She then announced that she was leaving us to get married. We were sad to lose her but happy for her. Now I needed someone who would live-in, look after the children, and help me run the big house. I had heard through friends that there was a family of Colombian women looking for work. Was I interested? I was. So one day Lucy came to our house. Lucy was a tall, round woman with an easy smile and a warm embrace. However, she did not speak a word of English, and my Spanish was elementary, but we understood each other, mixing words of Spanish, French, and Italian.

As soon as the children were settled in Elisabeth's guest house, I worked full-time for two months and then used every free moment to work on the book through the winter months. Jimmy who was always involved in my work, read the manuscript and drew all the illustrations. He created a cartoon of a boy/girl so that all the children could identify with the main character. By spring the book was finished, and I sent the manuscript to Lorraine. She loved it and went to work editing the book.

Around this time, I met Rita Reinhardt, the widow of the artist Ad Reinhardt. She came to me with a proposition. She was involved with a project called Art Park. Earl Brydges, state senator from Lewiston near Buffalo, had decided to put his town on the map by creating an art park there. The idea was that art should be a performance; it should come out to the open, out of the studio. Artists would go about creating their work in the park in full view of park visitors strolling along. Sometimes the public could even participate in the artist's work. Would I be interested, the following summer, in joining the group of artists that had been accepted? I would use food as my medium, and people would watch me create recipes. I would have a morning cooking class for children of the area. I would be paid for my work and housed. The list of artists was impressive, so I readily accepted. I was proud to be included as an artist.

The following July, with my son, Thomas, in tow, I drove to Buffalo and then on to Lewiston. The park was located on the Hudson River. It was a 200-acre park with a magnificent view of the gorge just beyond Niagara Falls. Along the pathways of the park were studios for artists. But during that first summer, the artists were working in makeshift studios. I was given a table, a hot plate, and nothing else. Nobody had prepared anything, so I went shopping in Buffalo. I bought everything I thought I would need for the children's cooking classes. I had read, in *The New York Times* about a month before, of a man who was importing a new gadget that he called "Cuisinart food processor" based on a French restaurant appliance. The electric utensil could mix, cut, shred, and beat. *The New York Times* called it a miracle machine . . . so I called Cuisinart in Connecticut and suggested that they send me a food processor. In exchange, I would demonstrate the appliance as I prepared food and would distribute pamphlets to the crowd. They agreed, and two days later I received my first food processor. I spent an entire day experimenting with the Cuisinart and found it very useful.

In those first few days of my arrival, I made it a point to meet the artists in residence. There was Catherine Jamison, a very intense young woman whose medium was photography. She printed her photographs on large white sheets that she spread on the grass so that the rays of the sun would be used like a catalyst. She befriended Thomas, who went around for her on his bicycle with a camera strapped to his ankles. Thomas's pictures of grass, insects, or paths would be developed to form an artistic pattern on those enormous sheets. Not far from where I was working was an artist who was building gigantic plastic forms, encouraging the public to join him in building forms that looked like enormous tinker toys. I met Charles Simmonds, a sculptor who built tiny cities in holes in the walls on the streets of New York. His miniature villages were made of bricks the size of grains of rice. He had a big project at Art Park. He was to build a house made with bags of earth filled with seeds. After rain, the house would sprout; corn and other vegetables would grow. However, in the morning he, like me, was to teach a group of children to make the tiny bricks he used in his art, so they could build their own cities. Neither he nor I, as yet, had any children for our classes. I suggested to the manager of Art Park that he should go on the radio and invite children to join us for a free cooking class and an art class. They would start with me then go on to Charles. It worked, and within days we both had a large group of children. I taught them the basics of cooking and made something they could eat for lunch. We made omelets, crêpes, grated carrot salad, sautéed chicken, rhubarb mousse, etc. While the children tried to cook, Bob Sacha, a young Lewiston photographer, took pictures of the children for the park. The food processor was a great help since in the afternoon I often had 100 people watching me create dishes that they all wanted to taste. In the late afternoon when the park closed, the artists would meet in one of the buildings. I often cooked for them or brought along dishes I had prepared in the afternoon. One day a week I took off with Thomas. We explored Niagara Falls or drove to Canada for dinner. Both Thomas and I had a great time. When we left Art Park, Catherine Jamison handed me a sheet with pictures of Thomas running around, playing, or helping her with her work. I framed the sheet, and to this day, it is hanging in our house.

Back in New York, the book *Cooking with Colette* was ready to go into print. The production people asked for a picture of me and kids cooking. I remembered that Bob Sacha had taken many pictures of us, so I asked him for one. He sent me a great photo of me looking on as a child tries to separate an egg. I wanted to use the picture for the cover of the book, but we needed signed consent forms to use it. Bob Sacha did not know who the little girl was. Hundreds of children had come to my stand in Art Park. How was I going to find her? Jimmy had a brilliant idea. We called the chief of police of Lewiston and asked for his help. We sent him the picture. Unfortunately, the police chief did not know who the girl was, but he sent it on to the local newspapers. The caption under the photograph in the local newspaper read, "Who Is This Mystery Child?" Within a few days, the little girl was found, and we were able to use her photo for the book.

Soon after *Cooking with Colette* was published, I received a telephone call from New American Library. The publisher had heard from Cuisinart that I had experimented with their food processor. Could I write a book about food processors, writing an evaluation of the best available, and develop a few recipes? By this time, I had switched from teaching at Hofstra University to St. Ann's School, a private school in Brooklyn that my own children attended. I was so busy with schoolwork that I asked a journalist friend, Jill Harris Herman, to help. I would test the food processors, take notes, and then she would write the evaluations while I developed recipes. My kitchen began to resemble an appliance store as I got inspired by the food processors, discovering that I could quickly prepare complicated dishes that, in the past, I had hesitated to prepare. Jill went to work, and Jimmy made line drawings of the processors and dishes. Within six months, we had a food processor cookbook and guide.

Meanwhile, Jill and I discovered that there were other well-known food writers writing food processor books, and I worried about the competition. Our book was called *A Mostly French Food Processor Cookbook,* and in the fall of 1977, the book came out with five others on the same subject! I was very scared, but thankfully the reviews were glowing. *The New York Times* called our book, "Outstanding. . . . Adventurous and inspired." We had a bestseller, and the book had to go back to press within one month. The publisher and I were very surprised by its success. Happily for me, it went into several printings. We sold over 100,000 copies within a year. I was interviewed on radio and television programs such as *Good Morning America.*

Although my articles, the cooking school, and *Cooking with Colette* had earned me a certain reputation in the food world, the success of this book opened new doors for me. My life was no longer the same. I started to meet other food writers and food critics. I was asked to lunches that, to my regret, I could rarely attend as I was still teaching; but my opinions on food and restaurants were sought out by people in the food world. I met Craig Claiborne, the esteemed restaurant critic of *The New York Times* who liked to come to dinner. He always brought interesting friends. Sometimes, I would see one of the dishes I had served him appear in his Saturday column. Once, at one of the dinners, he brought the stars of the famed TV show *Upstairs, Downstairs.* My children were in awe of these actors and hung in the staircase all during dinner, trying to catch glimpses of their favorite actors. The following Saturday, Craig wrote a profile of me, with the recipes for all the dishes I had served at dinner that night.

I also met Pierre Franey, who wrote a weekly column for *The New York Times.* When I met Gael Greene, she was a young food writer for *New York* magazine. We struck a friendship then. She often would call me to ask about new restaurants I had found in Chinatown. She was very generous and would always cite me as her source and give me credit. Sometimes I wrote articles for Dorothy Kalins of *Metropolitan Home,* and many others.

I also began to meet chefs and was often invited to the opening of new restaurants. In New York, I met Andre Soltner of Lutece; Barry Wines of The Quilted Giraffe, who, like me, loved Japanese and Chinese cuisines; Larry Forgione at River Café, whose American Cuisine taught me a lot; but it was with Alice Waters and Jeremiah Towers of Chez Panisse with whom I really identified. Alice believed in home grown ingredients, fresh and seasonal. She also brought California's attention to miniature vegetables, French string beans, local fish, and meats. For me they related to the way I actually cooked; they were the future in cooking. They also seemed to relate to what was happening in Europe, especially in France.

Worldwide, the best known chef at that time was Paul Bocuse of France. Paul Bocuse had trained in Fernand Point's restaurant La Pyramide and owned a three star restaurant in the outskirts of Lyon at Collonges-au-Mont-d'Or. Bocuse had just come out with a book in France called *La Cuisine du Marché,* which had revolutionized French cooking, then considered the best in the world. The book illustrated the way the new French chefs ran their restaurants and revolutionized their cuisine. They went to the market every morning and served only what was in season. The classic recipes of yesteryears were made lighter and more innovating. The book also discussed new trends among the French chefs: They all employed Japanese cooks in their kitchen and used Chinese techniques and utensils. In the United States, Pantheon bought the rights of Paul Bocuse's book and was looking for a translator.

I had met Paul Bocuse many years before on one of the food trips I had taken with my stepfather to La Pyramide. When Pantheon suggested me as a translator, Paul, who remembered meeting me and knowing my stepfather, agreed that I should translate the book. Bocuse's book contained 1,200 recipes; exhaustive step-by-step instructions to various methods of cooking; and sto-
nd his family. This was a monumental job! I had
ything like this before. I was still teaching full-
e of my four children, and running a very hectic
seemed too daunting, but I decided to take the
n anyway. The contract offered me two options: I

could get a substantial fee, or I could get a small fee with a share in the royalties. I consulted my agent and talked to my friends in the food world. Everyone agreed that this book was going to be a great success and that its sales would most probably top those of Julia Child, who was the reigning queen of the food world. I also learned that the first printing would be over 100,000 copies and that they predicted sales of over a million. I accepted the job and chose to share in the royalties. Working at night, I began to translate the book.

The first twenty pages seemed easy. Paul's style and explanations were clear and gave the reader tips that only a chef would know. But when I started to translate the recipes, I had the feeling that they were not Paul Bocuse's. Some assistant must have followed him as he cooked, then later adapted the recipes for household use. The problem was that whoever had written the recipes did not know how to cook. I was and am a cook that can easily detect, just by reading a recipe, if the recipe will or will not work. Many of Paul's recipes did not seem to work! Although I was denied a budget for testing, I decided to try some of the recipes in my own kitchen. The results were deplorable. I contacted Pantheon and suggested they send me to Lyon to talk over the recipes with Paul. The answer was a no; but I could telephone him and discuss them with him. I tried several times. Paul was either too busy or away and would refer me to his assistant who, I was sure, was the one who had written the book. Her responses were always the same: "Non, Madame Rossant, les recettes sont parfaites!" (No, Mrs. Rossant, the recipes are perfect!) I stopped calling after I translated the coq au vin recipe, which called for two quarts of red wine for a four-pound chicken. I had tested the recipe and found I had a coq au vin soup! Her answer to me was the same as usual. The recipe was correct. So I started to change the recipes but always writing explanations for the changes in the margins.

The book came out in the spring. Paul Bocuse, his wife, and his chefs de cuisine were put up at the Pierre Hotel. I was to meet Paul and accompany him to interviews and translate for him. Paul did not speak a word of English.

On the day of publication, Paul was to prepare a dinner at Lutece for the press. We were to meet for the first time in twenty-five years at 7:30 A.M. in front of Balducci's food store on Sixth Avenue to shop for the dinner. Paul had brought many things from France, but we needed meat, vegetables, and fruit. I recognized him immediately. Paul was a tall, imposing man with a prominent French nose and an easy smile. He embraced me heartily, nearly breaking all the bones in my back. A few journalists began to assemble, and Paul, acting like a great star, spoke with them as I, standing shyly behind him, translated their questions and his answers. Unfortunately, Balducci's had forgotten our appointment, and the store was not yet open; we were too early.

"Colette, I need breakfast; where shall we go?" I looked around. Nothing was open except McDonald's. I tried to explain that McDonald's, which had not as yet invaded France, was a fast-food chain, and there wasn't much he would like.

"Let's go there; it is fine," and so to McDonald's we went, followed by the press.

As we sat down, I explained to Paul what was on the menu. "You can have a muffin with egg and cheese, or ham."

"Muffin? What is a muffin?"

I explained, and Paul chose the muffin with eggs and ham and french fries. Paul ate the eggs with gusto, thought the coffee was too weak, but announced loudly that "These are the best french fries I have ever eaten. I want to meet the chef."

"But Paul, this is a fast-food restaurant, there is no chef."

"Nonsense Colette, every kitchen has a chef!"

With these words Paul got up and walked over to the counter where a young black man was standing, waiting to receive orders. To his astonishment and amidst flashes of the photographers, Paul insisted on shaking his hand and saying over and over again "Bravo, jeune homme. Les meilleures Frites que j'ai jamais mangées. Traduisez, Colette."

There were large headlines that evening in the papers, "Paul Bocuse eats the world's best french fries in New York at McDonald's."

The dinner at Lutece went well, and for the next two days, we ran around the city. Bocuse appeared on all the talk shows; always trailing behind, I was translating what he was saying. He loved American veal . . . believed our beef was the best in the world . . . he liked California wines, said their vegetables were great . . . but he missed French salad, bread, and butter.

On Wednesday, Pantheon received a call from Julia Child. She was opening Faneuil Hall in Boston with the mayor. She wanted Paul Bocuse to join her, and then they both would go to her home and together cook dinner for the press. Pantheon was in heaven. Julia Child, the grand dame of American food, was endorsing Paul Bocuse! Paul accepted, and I was told to call Julia Child and make the arrangements with her. We would both go to Boston, and I would continue to translate for him although Julia understood French very well. On Thursday, Paul received a call from the Rolex Watch Company. Would he pose for them on Friday for a rather substantial sum of money? Paul accepted and announced that he would forgo the trip to Boston. I pleaded with him, Pantheon pleaded, but Paul would not change his mind. I tried to explain who Julia Child was, how important she was to the American public, what she could do for the success or failure of his book. Nothing would budge him from his decision. He would not go and that was final!

I was told to call Julia Child and announce the bad news. Julia was furious with him and unfortunately with me, as the bearer of the bad news. The next day when interviewed on television about Faneuil Hall, Julia was asked what she thought of Paul Bocuse's cookbook. She dismissed it with shrug. "Nothing new," she said, "nothing worth talking about."

The book, which had sold 30,000 copies the first three days, had now slowed down to selling a trickle of copies. Our only hope was that with good publicity, the public would forget Julia Child's comments and again buy Paul Bocuse's book. This was not to happen because six months later an article appeared in *New York* magazine claiming that Paul Bocuse had never written the book. What he had done was buy the manuscript from the widow of a young, brilliant chef and adapted the young chef's recipes into his restaurant. Pantheon sued Flamarion, the French publisher. Bocuse accused us of not translating the foreword, which recounted the story of the manuscript. It turned out that the book that Flamarion sold to Pantheon was the second edition, and in that edition, there had been no foreword. Paul had not known what edition I had received. However, the book virtually stopped selling since the story made the rounds. My dreams of riches died with the book.

The following summer, Paul Bocuse, feeling sorry for me about what happened with the book, invited Jimmy and me to Lyon. He wrote, "I will send you off to visit all my friends: Troigros, Michel Guerard, and Outier. So come and see me." And so we did.

Bocuse's restaurant was just outside of Lyon. Paul received us in full chef regalia. We were given the royal treatment. He ordered all the recipes that had made him famous and that I had translated but never tasted. We had his signature soup—the one that he had made for the French president Giscard D'Estaing and that had earned him the title of Meilleur Ouvrier de France. The soup was called *soupe aux truffes Elysée,* a very strong flavored chicken consommé, with thick slices of black truffles swimming in it; the soup was sealed with a golden, buttery dome of flaky pastry. I broke the pastry dome, and suddenly I was engulfed in the truffles' strong, earthy aroma. This dish was followed by mullet served with a pistou sauce, then partridge with cabbage, and for dessert, the most beautiful croquette-en-bouche, tiny pâte à choux filled with cream and glazed with spun sugar. For the next two days, Paul took us around Lyon and talked about his pet project: an Oscar of food. (Three years later, true to his word, The Bocuse d'Or was born, and I was asked to be a judge for the first event.)

A few days later, going south, we stopped at Roanne at the Brother Troisgros's restaurant. Jean Troisgros was the younger brother. A handsome man who loved food, tennis, and architecture, Jean was in the process of remodeling his kitchen. When he discovered that Jimmy was an architect, he kidnapped him and while drinking 100-year-old Armagnac, discussed the remodeling of his restaurant. While they were occupied, I was told to go to the kitchen to observe how a famous kitchen was run. The kitchen staff put me in a corner near a giant stainless steel vat filled with boiling water. I looked around and was astonished by the noise and the speed with which everyone cooked. Then I turned my attention to the vat. I wondered, as I looked around, what the vat was for. Soon I understood it was for making the consommé used in cooking. Every bone, every leftover raw vegetable went in the vat. The young chefs would throw chicken bones from their cooking station, like a basketball player throwing a ball. They never missed! What made this vat different from the others I had seen before was that this one had its own stove and was gargantuan. At the bottom of the vat was a faucet. From time to time, a young apprentice would come and first remove the scum that was building on top, adding salt and freshly ground pepper, then retrieve some broth for the chef de cuisine. At night the broth was strained, degreased, and used for preparing Trois-gros famous *Filet de Boeuf au bouillon de Pot-au-Feu* (a piece of beef poached in this strong delectable consommé), which we were served at dinner that night. The meat was so tender one could cut it with a fork.

Once Jimmy had visited the architect in charge of the remold-ing of the restaurant and given some suggestions, we left for Saulieu to visit Bernard Loiseau's La Côte d'Or restaurant with a care package of homemade sausages, fresh bread, and a bottle of Troisgros's best wine.

Bernard Loiseau was also young, but less of star than Bocuse and more of a family man than Jean Troisgros. In Loiseau's restau-rant we talked about his children and ours. I felt very much at home with him. We dined on breast of chicken poached with truf-fles surrounded with slices of foie gras, so rich and tender that I can still taste it. The rest of the meal is a blur. The next day we drove to Michel Guerard in the Bordeaux region at Les Près D'Eugenie hotel and restaurant. Michel Guerard, like Paul Bo-cuse, was a star. He was very proud of his hotel and restaurant and felt strongly that like Bocuse a few years before, he had come up with a new and revolutionary way of cooking. Cuisine Minceur was his contribution to the new woman, and giving me a mean-ingful look, he said he hoped I would try it. He promised me that his menu Minceur (a gourmet diet menu) would allow me to shed the few pounds I had acquired in my quest for good food. I had a poached sole in a very light broth and delicate miniature vegeta-bles that simply disappeared in one bite. Dessert was a fruit souf-flé with just egg whites. If I could cook that way, I would certainly go on his diet.

Jimmy opted for the regular restaurant dinner and splurged on rabbit and Guerard's famous cannelloni with herbs. I was jealous of Jimmy, who raved of his meal all the way to our next stop.

Before going on to Outier's restaurant in the South of France, I needed to rest from all this rich food. We drove to Hendaye, a small town on the Atlantic coast, where thirty years ago, Jimmy had proposed to me in front of an old-fashioned hardware store. To our disappointment, it was now a very modern one. A few days later, rested, we went on to Outier.

L'Oasis, Outier's restaurant, was a beautiful place near the ocean in the small town of La Napoule near Cannes. This was to be the end of our trip. Outier was more like Jean Troisgros. He was tall, very handsome, and believed himself to be the best cook in France. He was very proud of his three-star Michelin rating. Outier was one of the first chefs that I had met who was truly international. He had opened restaurants in Thailand and India. That night, I told Outier what we had done and eaten for the last ten days. He then understood that to conquer us and show me what a great chef he was, he had to serve us something lovely, but simply cooked because by now, I could no longer eat and wished only for plain yogurt! He served us a frothy consommé, light as air, with tiny morsels of fresh raw scallops. This was followed by the best bouillabaisse I had ever tasted. Just before the next dish arrived, to clear our pallet, a small pear and brandy sorbet was placed in front of us. The cool sorbet was so refreshing that suddenly I felt rejuvenated and with enjoyment, ate the roast squab that followed. Later, while I was savoring a fresh *fromage blanc* drizzled with local honey and roasted walnuts, Outier talked about coming to New York and opening a new restaurant. He had trained a young chef who would run the restaurant while Outier was at L'Oasis. Outier, three years later, true to his word, opened Lafayette, a restaurant in the Drake Hotel in New York. He brought with him the young chef whom he had trained. Jean-

Georges Vongerichten, like his mentor, would become the darling of New York and one of the United States best-known chefs. He would also open restaurants around the world.

A few days later, we were back in New York, and I contemplated all I had seen and learned during those two weeks traveling in France. The chefs I had visited had served us smaller portions than the usual ones served in New York restaurants. Garnishes had changed. Fresh edible flowers were now used as garnishes, and the plates were very large and often made of glass instead of china. Soufflés, salty or sweet, were made with no flour, and flavored oils were drizzled on vegetables. Steaming and poaching, it seemed to me, were now the rule. Fresh fava beans, tiny artichokes, shredded leeks, snow peas, and sugar snap peas were the vegetables of choice. Desserts had also changed. For the first time, I ate an oriental persimmon mousse topped with pomegranate juice in a French restaurant. Gone were the heavy cakes; they were replaced with strange tasting ginger sorbets or ice creams flavored with black pepper. Jean-Georges made potato chips with beets and served pig cheeks as a main course. Oriental vegetables appeared in menus, and sesame seeds seemed to be in every dish. Slowly my own way of cooking changed. As I was now teaching in Brooklyn, I often, after work, walked across the Brooklyn Bridge into Chinatown. I would shop there for our evening meal. I discovered that Chinese butchers carried, as I had seen in French open markets, wild ducks, tiny quails, very young chickens, and thins slices of beef or pork that one could cook in a few seconds. Vegetables in Chinese grocery stores were always seasonal and very fresh. Asparagus were thick and tender; there was tiny bok choy, snow pea leaves, and sweet potato leaves that were better than the regular supermarket spinach.

Every night I experimented with new recipes. I started to consider every aspect of a dish: color, texture, overall presentation, as well as the star attraction, taste. I began jotting down recipes I had developed, like a stuffed lemon braised with tiny pearl onions or Brussels sprouts rolled in sesame seeds. Very soon I had a stack of them. I wanted to write a new cookbook. This one would contain my very own recipes and would be based on the way we lived. I wanted to write for the working parents who, when they came home, were faced with children clamoring for dinner and no time to spend on long arduous recipes. I really believed that there was no reason why a working woman or man could not turn the kitchen into a place for high adventure. I knew it could be done.

My book would be called, *Colette Rossant's After Five Gourmet.* "After Five" because most people left their workplaces at five. I suggested in my book that they shop on their way home and give themselves two hours to prepare and serve dinner. Recipes would be classified by ingredients and time. You could prepare hors d'oeuvres in less than fifteen minutes with ricotta and fines herbs on toasted round bread or a mushroom flan. There were recipes for beef, chicken, or fish that took thirty minutes to overnight depending on the time you had on your hands. At that time I was teaching at St. Ann's. I was in charge of organizing exchange programs abroad for our students and heading the foreign language department. I had ten teachers to help and many problems to solve. I was running a household and helping my own children with their homework. Despite all these responsibilities, I managed to serve dinners every night following the principles of this new book.

The After-Five Gourmet came out in the fall of 1981. While the book did not become a bestseller like the food processor cookbook, I believed it was the best cookbook I had ever written. I still believe it today.

For the next three years, although I continued to write articles about food and do restaurant reviews, I just didn't think I had another cookbook in me. But one morning, I received a call from a friend. Her daughter was getting married, and to my friend's dismay, she was marrying into a very orthodox Jewish family. Although my friend was Jewish, her family was secular and disliked traditional Kosher food. Furthermore, most of her daughter's friends were also nonobservant.

"Colette, you have to help me. You must devise the wedding menu and prepare it in the hall's Kosher kitchen, where the wedding will take place."

"Impossible; I can't. I know nothing about Kosher cuisine."

"I will give you the name of a rabbi; he will help you and teach you what you can and cannot serve. You will invent new dishes. I know you can do it. Please, Colette, don't let me down!"

During the next few weeks, I trotted down to the Jewish Seminary to talk to the rabbis there about my menu, and what I could serve and what I could not. The major challenge for me was that I could not use any dairy with the meal. I had never cooked without butter or cream.

For a few weeks, I worked in the kitchen, buying meat and poultry at Kosher butchers. I had discovered in Chinatown a new bean curd, very light, very creamy. So I went back to the Seminary to ask if the rabbis thought I could use bean curd. *Was it Kosher? Could I serve it at a meal that included meat?* A few days later, I received the answer: Yes, I could replace cream in recipes with this bean curd.

I went back to work, and by the end of the month, I had a menu ready. It was approved by the bride and her mother; I wrote down the recipes for the catering kitchen and waited anxiously for the big day.

The wedding day finally came. After the traditional ceremony, drinks were served, accompanied by cherry tomatoes filled with my own versions of chopped chicken liver and mushrooms stuffed with baked salmon and capers. At this point, though, there was too much excitement for anyone to notice the food. Then we all sat down to dinner. Some eyebrows were raised when the appetizer arrived: stuffed smoked salmon with asparagus puree, followed by a veal pate on a bed of endives.

When the main course came along, a shoulder of lamb with Japanese *shiso* leaves served with a julienne of young vegetables and fresh noodles in a mushroom sauce or fresh whole red snapper stuffed with fennel, I heard murmurs. Just before the dessert, toasts were made by family and friends; then the rabbi who had officiated got up, and after toasting the bride and the groom, called for a round of applause for the cook: "This was the best wedding dinner I have ever had!" said the rabbi as he raised his glass to me. Everyone relaxed and joined in. I had succeeded. The wedding dinner had been a strictly Kosher meal. It had been elegant, light, and very much "Nouvelle Cuisine." By the time dessert was served, a tower of tiny baked choux filled with a raspberry puree and enveloped in a net of spun sugar, dozens of wedding guests approached me asking for recipes.

A few days later, I received a call from an editor at Arbor House, a small publishing house in Manhattan. "I was a guest at the wedding you catered," he said. "I was very taken by your work and would like to talk to you about doing a Kosher cookbook."

When we met, he told me that there was a tremendous religious revival taking place across the United States. Many young Jews were tracing their roots and yearning for family, tradition, and a sense of belonging, but with added sophistication. The newly observant people knew what good food was; they were au courant when it came to eating. Their knowledge of wines was impressive, their taste in food refined, yet they had an unwavering determination to respect Jewish dietary laws, and this is where I came in. "I want you to write a cookbook expressing the 'new Jewish cuisine.'" We are a small company, and I cannot give you a large advance. I can pay you for the recipes and give a larger than usual share in the profits. This book will be a great success."

Why did I agree to these terms? I don't know, probably for the challenge of creating something new. And so I went to work. Every week I sent recipes to the Jewish Seminary, to be sure that there would be no mistakes. The book was published in the spring of 1986, and we all waited to see the miracle of everyone rushing to buy the book, but this failed to happen. My Kosher cookbook was too untraditional, especially facing the new revival of orthodoxy.

The press ignored the book, the public did not buy it, and the publisher went bankrupt. Once again I had lost! I swore I would never again write another cookbook.

However, the future proved me wrong. In the next few years, because of my travels and my adventures, I would write three more cookbooks, two memoirs, and the book you are reading now.

≽≼

POACHED SALMON WITH SPINACH TARRAGON SAUCE

Heat 6 cups of water in a deep skillet; add 1 sliced carrot, 1 small onion stuck with 2 garlic cloves, 1 bay leaf, and 5 peppercorns. Bring to a boil, lower the heat to medium, and cook for 10 minutes.

Then add 4 salmon steaks. Bring the liquid to a boil again, lower the heat to medium, and cook for 10 more minutes.

Remove the salmon steak on to a platter. Reserve the cooking liquid.

In a blender or food processor, place 1 cup of fresh tarragon leaves; 2 cups of fresh spinach, stems removed; and 1 cup of watercress, stems removed. Add 3 tablespoons of olive oil, 1 tablespoon of lemon juice, and 1 cup of the poached salmon broth. Process until all the ingredients are pureed. Remove to a bowl, add salt and pepper to taste, and serve with the salmon steaks.

Serves 4.

ROAST QUAILS

Preheat oven to 375°.

In a bowl, mix together 2 tablespoons of soy sauce with 2 table-spoons of olive oil and 2 tablespoons of grated fresh ginger. Rub 8 quails with the soy mixture. Place 1 kumquat and 1 thyme sprig in the cavity of the quails. Sprinkle with salt and pepper to taste. Place the quails side by side in a baking pan. Add 2 cups of chicken bouillon to the pan, and bake the quails for 35 minutes or until quails are golden brown.

Serves 4.

Discovering the delights of Japan

6

The Travels

$$\Longrightarrow\Longleftarrow$$

Travel had become one of my passions. Every winter I would dream of places to go when school was over. I wanted to see the world, and I wanted my children to share in my experiences. In fact, Jimmy and I traveled mostly with the children; but sometimes it would just be Jimmy and I.

One summer we went to Guatemala with our four children, camped in cheap motels, and discovered the great wonders of the Mayan cities. Another trip took us to France. Once there, I convinced my mother and stepfather that a trip to Spain would do wonders for my mother's rheumatism, so Jimmy and I drove the two of them over the Pyrenees. One summer, Jimmy was invited to Rio de Janeiro and Sao Paulo in Brazil, to give a series of lectures. I insisted he take me with him, saying that I spoke the language and that I could translate for him. "What about the children?" he asked. "Lucy," my faithful housekeeper, was my answer.

Jimmy and I went to Brazil for three weeks, leaving the children with Lucy in East Hampton. The trip was fascinating. I loved the town of Manaus on the Amazon, with its markets and old colonial buildings. I thought that Brasília, the new capital, had fantastic architecture, but was too empty and grandiose. Then we visited Rio de Janeiro, with its lovely beaches, and went on to Sao Paulo. Jimmy was lecturing at the university, while I roamed the markets that were run by Japanese immigrants or strolled on Sao Paulo's main streets, stopping at small stands selling delicacies that I had not tasted since I had left Cairo. Sao Paulo had a large Arab population, and the city smelled of cumin and garlic. I was in heaven.

I came back enamored of South America. The summer had been a success; Lucy and the children loved East Hampton, so the following year, at Lucy's urging, we went to Colombia for a visit. We stopped first at Cartagena, a teeming colonial port, then went on to Lucy's village of Santa Catarina where we became acquainted with her big family, including her son. The village was quite poor. Most of the houses were made of mud, except Lucy's house, which towered above the others and was made of brick. All the money she earned taking care of us went to her family and the house. We all sat in the garden, told of how wonderful Lucy was, ate mangoes and plantains, and then laden with presents for Lucy and the children, we flew to Bogotá, Villa de Leyva, Popayán, and Medellín.

By now, times were difficult. New York was in the throes of a serious recession and Jimmy's office had lost several important projects. Marianne was starting her first year in college; Juliette was a senior in high school and applying to colleges. Cecile was a junior and Thomas was about to enter the fifth grade. In a year we would have two children in college, and we were both quite worried. Money would be scarce, and the colleges my children were applying to were very expensive. I looked for more free-lance work and Jimmy, hoping to sell some of his drawings, searched for a gallery that would show his work.

The following year, Juliette was accepted at Dartmouth College, and Marianne transferred to New York University. Our fears were realized, we now had two children in private universities. This time fate was on our side and help came in a very unusual way.

One evening, two years later, while we were having dinner, Jimmy announced that Habitat, an arm of the United Nations, wanted an architect to go to Tanzania and review the design for the central part of the planned new capital, called Dodoma. The plan, prepared by a Canadian firm, had pleased no one. The President of Tanzania did not like it, nor did the UN experts who reviewed its design. Tanzania? Where was Tanzania? We rushed to an atlas. Tanzania, Thomas read with awe, was far away in East Africa, near Zanzibar and between Kenya and Uganda. Thomas read that Swahili was the national language, although everyone in school had to learn English, and that Tanzania had a Socialist government with a leader called Julius Nyerere. We all looked at Jimmy. *Would he apply for the job?* Jimmy looked at me. He saw in my face that I was worried. This was a winter trip, I worked, and the children were in school. "It is only for three months," he said. We had never been separated for more than a week in almost twenty years! *Three months?* "Of course you must apply," I said, trying to be a good wife. "It sounds so exciting." I was petrified.

In early September, Jimmy left for Tanzania. I heard from him at least once a week.

"Are you happy? How is the work?"

"Difficult. The country is fascinating and very beautiful. There are lots of problems with the Canadians. Food is terrible, English, bland, and very little of it."

"What problems? Are you OK?"

"Can't explain on the phone, I will write and . . ."

The telephone would go dead. This happened again and again and was very frustrating. On the phone, I could never tell Jimmy what was happening here in New York. He hadn't asked how I was or about the children, nor did he answer pressing questions, such as "the bathroom on the top floor is leaking; what do I do; who do I call?"

In late October, I received a letter from Jimmy saying that the job was exciting; the plan they were reviewing was, as predicted, not very good. He was drawing a lot; he had befriended some of the Tanzanian planners and was working hard.

A few days later he called. "Listen, I met the president. We got along; he is a very interesting man. He has gray hair like me. By the way, I don't think I will be able to be back for Christmas."

"What, what did you say?"

"There is too much work."

And once again the telephone went dead.

Not back for Christmas? Had I heard correctly? I was crushed; Christmas was a very important holiday for me. As a child in Cairo, I always dreamt of spending Christmas with my mother, but it never happened. When Marianne was born, I promised myself to always be there for Christmas, and to have a tree with lots of presents under it. Up to that day, I had kept that promise. But now without Jimmy, Christmas would not be the same. I was very upset.

Suddenly, a week before Christmas, Jimmy called and asked me to join him. He had a few days off, and he would love it if I came. *Leave New York and the children? Who would take care of Cecile and Thomas? Could I really go and leave them alone for ten days?* When

I asked my oldest daughter, Marianne, who was home from college for the holidays, what she thought, she said, "Don't be ridiculous! I will be here, and there is Lucy. Juliette and I will take care of everything. We can celebrate Christmas a couple of days before, and then you can go." A few days before Christmas, as soon as school let out, we bought a tree and decorated it. On the evening of the twenty-second, I placed all the presents under the tree, and we all opened them the next morning. At night, bundled up in my winter clothes and heavy boots, carrying a suitcase filled with summer clothes and food, and after many speeches, hugs, and good-byes to the children and Lucy, I left via London for Tanzania. I arrived in Dar es Salaam on Christmas morning, laden with gifts that Jimmy had requested—canned pates, tuna, sardines, packages of cookies and cakes, and a bra for the wife of one of the officials in Dodoma. I had roamed New York City looking for that bra—a size 44 DD!

The Dar es Salaam airport seemed primitive; a large wooden structure, open on all sides. Luggage was carried by hand to and from the planes. After going through customs and a passport check, I looked for my luggage and Jimmy. I found neither. Women in brightly colored wraps and men in khaki-colored safari suits were moving around seemingly without purpose, unaffected by the confusion, the damp heat, the noise. In my winter coat and boots, I felt faint from the heat. What should I do if he did not show up? I knew no one here. Finally, I saw Jimmy running to greet me. "Sorry, sorry . . . I was in a meeting . . . forgot the time," he panted. His embrace soothed me, but I had to tell him the bad news. "No luggage . . . it's lost." Jimmy looked around, found an airline official, and displaying his UN credentials, he asked for help. "No problem, Mzee Jim, we will find it soon and bring it to the hotel. No problem!" *No problem* was an expression I would hear time and time again in Tanzania.

We were informed that our cookie-cutter hotel, ten stories high with balconies overlooking a boulevard, had no hot water until late afternoon. I needed a shower desperately, but I had to wait, so Jimmy took me for a walk around town. The streets smelled vaguely of gasoline and fried food, but my hunger overcame my slight nausea. Jimmy said that the best food in Dar was Indian. As we sat down in an open-air Indian café, I looked at him. In the past three months, he had changed a lot. In New York, he was often tense, nervous, and worried. Today, he seemed relaxed, joyful and smiling. He looked so comfortable, so at home in this little Indian restaurant. He had lost weight and looked at least ten years younger. I smiled at him, happy to see him so well, and as I munched on tiny delicious samosas, fried dough filled with spicy meat and potatoes, I listened to his chatter. He explained that a very large Indian population had been imported to Tanzania when the English were building the East African railroad system. He had many Indian friends in Dodoma. While he ordered the next dish, a highly seasoned chicken curry, more sauce than chicken, and an excellent ice-cold Tanzanian beer, bottled in unlabeled brown glass, he told me that the calculators he had asked me to bring were for them. The Indians in Dodoma were Sikhs and were in the construction business. I learned that trouble was brewing between the Canadian team, who had developed the plan, and the Tanzanians. "Let's have some dessert, *la specialité de la maison*," he said mockingly. It was something that I had never seen before, bright orange twirls of deep-fried dough soaking in honey. More beer please . . . this was pure sugar!

Back at the hotel, there was no suitcase and no hot water. I removed my boots and my pantyhose full of runs and rinsed my swollen feet in cool water. We were going to have dinner with George Kahama, Director of the CDA (Capital Development Authority) and his wife. What about shoes? Could I at least buy some shoes? Out again, down to the main shopping street. As I looked at the shoe stores, I realized that all the shoes had five- to six-inch heels, most of them platform. I tried several pairs and finally settled on one that didn't seem as high, and out I went, tottering as if I were walking on eggs, but certainly better off than in heavy winter boots. Kahama arrived on time, a small, charming, and rotund man, with an easy laugh, wearing an elegant safari suit. His wife was twice his size, beautiful, with a regal bearing. I realized then that the bra was for her. She was wearing a long flowing white dress, and around her shoulders was draped a yellow and green kente cloth with political slogans all over it. The effect was stunning. I told my sad story: no suitcase, no clothes. She smiled and said it would come back to me, "No problem!"

The next morning a package for me arrived at the hotel. Inside was a long, blue dress, much like the one Kahama's wife wore. A hand-written note said that her dressmaker had made it that night for me and that she hoped it would fit me. She hoped I would find my suitcase soon. I am sure I did not look as beautiful as she did, but I was thankful for being able to change into clean clothes.

The city's dilapidated houses, the broken sidewalks, the children walking barefoot, and the beggars all disturbed me. But I was in awe of the fish market, sprawled on a sandy beach near the harbor. Thin, shirtless men were calling out to shoppers to view their enormous kingfish, prawns, and sharks. One vendor was cooking prawns in a huge wok-like pan over an open fire. Jimmy walked by my side, at ease with the scene, explaining that President Nyerere, a Socialist leader, had transformed the country by making education mandatory and by regrouping the population into new villages, each built around a central square with a clinic, party headquarters, and a school. But the country was still very poor, and corruption in Dar es Salaam, he told me solemnly, was rampant. Nyerere hoped to change this by moving the capital to Dodoma, now a village in the country's interior, without Dar's constant physical reminders of Tanzania's colonial past. Nyerere felt that setting the capital in the center would help the poorest areas in the country develop.

Back at the hotel, I called the airline for my suitcase. "No problem," said the man who answered. "We'll send it to Dodoma on the next plane." That afternoon we flew to Dodoma.

Dodoma had once been a railway junction between Dar es Salaam and Uganda's capital, Kampala. The Germans had built the railroad and Dodoma, which was then just a small junction town. Much later, the English had enlarged the station and built the hotel where we were staying. The hotel was lovely with low-lying buildings surrounding a magnificent, arcaded courtyard with flowering trees and exotic plants. There were little tables in the shade for afternoon tea and drinks. I felt as if I were part of a Masterpiece Theater series about colonial East Africa.

Jimmy told me what was happening with the new capital plans and his job. Over the past two months, Jimmy had analyzed the plans for the future capital, pointing out all its mistakes. He had also drawn a preliminary plan of his own, which had impressed Kahama, his team of young Tanzanian planners, and even the president. "Now," Jimmy explained, "I have to resign from the job, go back to New York, and reapply as the planner for the city downtown. I will then be able to bring my own team." What about me? "Well," Jimmy said with excitement in his voice, "you could come with Thomas for three months in the summer and stay here with him in Dodoma. The government would give us a large house with a servant, and it would be a marvelous vacation for both of you."

The next day, while Jimmy was in meetings, I roamed around the small town. Low-lying buildings and arcades that housed small shops surrounded Dodoma's main square: a restaurant here and there, a tire place, a garage, and two Indian grocery stores. I went into one of the grocery stores; most of the shelves were almost empty, with just a few cans, some vegetables, soap, and sprays for cockroaches. Beyond the grocery was a beauty salon. As I looked through the glass, I saw women who had their hair done in very intricate braids, a fashion that would hit New York years later. Their hair was beautiful; each woman seemed to have a different design. What patience they had!

Next to the beauty salon was an Indian sweet shop offering desserts much like the one I had in Dar es Salaam; further down was a small store, a hole in the wall, selling fried samosas and other Indian dishes. At one corner of the square was a stand selling tiny pieces of liver on skewers and roasted tiny bananas. I tried a couple of bananas and was quite surprised; they were so sweet, and their strong aroma was intoxicating. Near the center of town were large villas built by the English after World War I. They now housed expatriates working on the new capital. A little further from the center were simple, one-story stucco houses with red tiled roofs that Tanzanians and Indians lived in—those, of course, who owned businesses. Several villages of Wagogo (Dodoma's local tribe, Kahama's people who lived in sunken mud houses), surrounded Dodoma. When I recounted what I had done during the day, Jimmy told me that about ten miles out of town were encampments of Masai, a tribe who raised large herds of goats and cows. The town had a country club, left over from the British colonials, with a swimming pool and tennis courts. Today the club's members were Tanzanians who had come from Dar es Salaam to work on the capital project and wealthy Indians and expats who came from Scandinavia, England, France, and Germany.

That night we ate in a garden restaurant with an enormous grill. Small, scrawny chickens, marinated for an entire day in lime juice, hot peppers, ginger, and cloves, were broiled and served with grilled bananas and beer. I was famished and gobbled the moist, lean chicken flesh. I can say now, without a doubt, that the Tanzanian way of preparing fowl is the best I've ever discovered in all my travels. I was so enchanted by the way they cooked the chicken, that later on I used that recipe in one of my cookbooks.

A few days later, I flew back to Dar es Salam. Jimmy told me he would resign in a few weeks and fly back to New York to wait for the president and Kahama to apply to the UN for his return. As I boarded the plane to New York, "No problem" were the last words I heard. The suitcase turned up two months later after a wonderful vacation.

Once back in New York, Jimmy waited impatiently for a word from the UN. *Would he go back to Dodoma and design the center of the new capital?* Six months went by before he received the hoped-for answer. Jimmy and Thomas were jubilant. Thomas insisted that we all take Swahili lessons before the summer.

For the next three weeks, I saw little of Jimmy. He had to choose a team to go with him, and he worked day and night on the preliminary design of the capital. He selected two young architects: John Diebboll, a soulful, quiet twenty-three-year-old who seemed almost to worship his boss, and Tom Anderson, more experienced than John, and quite ambitious, and a few others as well. They all left at the end of March with the promise that I would follow with Thomas in June. Marianne, home from college, would hold the fort in New York, along with my intrepid Lucy. The end of June arrived very quickly, and now it was our turn to suffer a slew of shots and quinine pills. Jimmy's letters were full of requests: bring food (there was very little in

Dodoma) like canned beans, sugar, flour, powdered milk, and spices. Don't forget makeup, lots of it, cheap calculators, utility candles, and over-the-counter medicines. Stop in Paris and buy a bicycle for Thomas, along with fresh butter, cheese, cookies, and crackers. A letter would arrive every week with new requests. I ordered a food processor with a transformer and stocked up on shampoo. At the airport, we looked like refugees leaving New York forever.

The plane from Paris to Dodoma stopped in Ethiopia for a couple of hours. As we left the plane, I was told by an airline official that Thomas and I could not go back on the plane because they needed our seats for a Chinese delegation. I stood there dumbfounded. We would have to stay in Addis Ababa for two to three days until another plane came. Sitting on a hard plastic airport chair, I looked at Thomas, whose lanky legs were drawn up to his chin, patiently waiting. I suddenly had an idea. I whispered to him, "Throw yourself on the floor and start moaning. Say you are very sick and try to throw up." Thomas was so convincing that the manager of the airline, fearing that something terrible would happen to my son, decided to put us back on the plane in first class!

The house in Dodoma was spare, airy, and large, with two bedrooms, a living/dining room, and a simple kitchen with an electric range and a refrigerator. The sink had only one faucet for cold water. The bathroom was rudimentary, but the house was bright and very breezy. There was a lovely garden with an avocado tree and a papaya tree. Jimmy had chosen a young Tanzanian in his early twenties to help us with the house. Simon (many Tanzanians have two names, one English and one Swahili) would clean, take care of the garden, and help me in any way I wanted. He lived two hours away and walked to our house every morning. I stored the butter and cheeses from Paris and the bread and vegetables from the Dar market in the refrigerator. Our first night there, we took Thomas to the chicken restaurant for dinner. Thomas loved it and decided that Dodoma was a great place to be until we returned home and found the house in darkness. No more electricity! The butter had already melted in the late afternoon heat; we had to find a cool place for the cheeses and the vegetables. We lit candles and undressed in semi-darkness.

"When will electricity come back?" I asked.

Jimmy smiled. "I don't know. The roads from Dar es Salaam are flooded, and the new electric generator is stuck in the harbor. This is a poor country, but don't worry we will manage quite well."

I lay next to Jimmy on our thin mattress, somewhat incredulous that we were living in this tiny African village. Suddenly, I heard a light thud on our bed, as if something had fallen from the ceiling. I screamed, Jimmy lit a candle, and we looked down. On the sheet were two small lizards, light green and about four-inches long; six more were still clinging to the ceiling. Jimmy tried to reassure me.

"Don't be afraid . . . relax, Colette . . . they're harmless."

"I hate lizards and large bugs."

"But these are very friendly; in fact, they eat the bugs that would hurt you."

With this statement, he swept our new friends off our blanket.

For the next few weeks, I would count the lizards on the ceiling before I closed my eyes. If they were only a few—three or four—I'd fall asleep, but if there were more, I had a hard time. A few days later, when I admitted to Simon that I was afraid of lizards, he made a point of removing most of the lizards with a broom just before he left the house. I was grateful for this.

Over the next three months, electricity came on a couple of

hours a day or not at all. We learned to go to bed at dusk and rise with the sun. We also learned to read by candlelight. We took turns, one reading aloud to the other two. If Lincoln had done it, Thomas reasoned, then why couldn't we?

Preparing meals was another problem; one that, in retrospect, taught me a great deal about how to be both resilient and creative when cooking. The electric range, of course, was useless. Simon bought us a small, locally made charcoal stove (a cylinder of tin), and every morning he came from his village with a bag of charcoal and twigs and lit a fire for our breakfast, repeating this indispensable service at lunch and dinner. I tried to replicate his actions several times, but had no luck lighting the stove.

What to cook? Every day Dodoma's Central Square had a market. Farmers would come from around Dodoma, but there was very little to buy. Vendors squatted on the dusty ground in front of their produce: a few piles of eggplant (three to a pile); tomatoes, again three to a pile; tiny, sweet mangoes; cherimoyas; and dried fish (infested with flies) from the river. Then there were mountains of *ugali*, the maize that Tanzanians cooked like polenta; there also tiny potatoes; these turned out to be delicious. What I needed most was oil, butter, and especially bread. There was one baker in town, a Greek who had lived in Dodoma for forty years. Every day, as I entered the store, he would say, "None today. Tomorrow there'll be bread. No problem." We went days at a time without bread. Chickens were small and sold live. If I wanted one, I had to kill it myself. One day I gave in, bought a chicken, and took it home, holding the squirming bird by its feet. I went out to the back yard, called Thomas for moral support, and cut its neck with my one sharp knife by holding its body between my knees. I screamed like a wounded animal as I did the deed. Then I had to eviscerate it! All my years of cooking hadn't prepared me for this. How do you pluck a chicken without pulling off all the skin with the feathers? I should have brought the *Joy of Cooking* with me; it would have helped, I'm sure. I felt like a pioneer's wife who had not married into her own class. And I rather enjoyed the disgusting romance of it!

That night we ate dry, skinless, grilled chicken, but it was better than another can of sardines. We hadn't had meat in almost a week. There *was* a butcher on the square, of course. But his chunks—I wondered if he'd torn them off—of goat and beef were plagued with buzzing flies and hung drearily in rows on metal hooks. When I asked for a pound, I got half a pound of meat along with another half pound of fat, gristle, and bone. An expatriate neighbor, a bird-like English woman, advised me that if I cooked the meat until it was overdone, the flies didn't matter. But I just could not make myself buy this meat again.

For the next few days, we survived on eggs, but our life changed when I was told about the Saturday Market. It was located near the slaughterhouse on a dusty plain near a small creek outside of Dodoma. It was a market where the Masai brought their lambs, goats, and calves to be slaughtered. Crouching in the dirt were women selling brilliantly colored cloth that they wrapped around their bodies, sometimes even over cotton, American-style dresses. There were stands for wooden bowls; dark, glossy shepherds' clubs carved from single branches of a tree; enameled cooking utensils; and flat leather thongs. But most of all, Saturday Market was for live and butchered goats, sheep, and cattle from the slaughterhouse. The very first Saturday I visited the market, I made an ally in Philip, a short wiry young butcher who sold small goats from a wooden stand. For a few minutes, I watched him cutting up goats with a machete-like knife, like the butchers at the daily market in Dodoma's Central Square. Suddenly I had an idea. I proposed a plan that would benefit us both: I'd teach him how to butcher the goats the European way, and he would gain expatriate clients willing to pay a much higher price for the meat. Philip agreed and told me to meet him the next day. As I drove our dusty white Peugeot station wagon (a vehicle ubiquitous in East Africa) to the slaughterhouse, I hoped that I really knew how to carve a goat. After all, I was French and remembered the proper French cuts of lamb and beef. Furthermore, I had often cut up chickens or deboned a duck. I also remembered the diagram of a cow with the different pieces of meat so well-defined in Fanny Farmer's cookbook. *Could butchering a goat be very much different?* To the rear of Philip's stand, I found a whole goat splayed on the table. Philip handed me a machete with a long, curved, menacing blade. I told Philip that I would guide him, but that he would have to do the cutting himself. The lessons began.

"First," I said, "cut the goat in half lengthwise, following the backbone." This exposed the liver, which I pulled out still warm, my hand shaking. I then told him to remove the entrails. Hoping not to feel too sick, I turned away while he did that. I looked for the kidneys and wasn't very sure where they were, but once he removed the entrails, I saw them and knew that the European expatriates, especially the British, would love them and told Philip that. Then I carefully showed him how to carve the leg (it would be delicious broiled), and the small chops from the upper ribs. I was speaking to him as if in a trance, allowing instinct to guide me. Philip seemed to transform himself almost spiritually into a butcher-artist. He went at the shoulder with intense focus while he listened to my directions to cut the meat into even cubes for stew and showed professional pleasure as he carved out the small, tender-looking filet. We cut up two goats that day. As I left, I reminded him to keep the filet and the liver for me, which I'd promised to buy each Saturday. I also promised that if he butchered the goat the new way from now on, I would tell all the expatriates in town to buy exclusively from him. Back home, I marinated the filet in lime juice, thyme, and local pepper and broiled it on our charcoal stove. We ate tender roasted goat with small potatoes. It was the best home dinner we had had in weeks. The next day I invited Jimmy's team to dinner, and, after marinating the liver in vinegar, lime juice, and a small green leaf that tasted like lemon that I found in the market (to this day, I don't know what it was), I broiled it and served it with onions and tomatoes.

The next day, as I had promised Philip, I went visiting. Obliged to drink endless cups of tea and nibble on stale biscuits after I knocked on each expatriate's door, I managed to notify most of our neighborhood about Philip's specially butchered meat. The following Saturday, I arrived at the market and saw an actual line of people waiting to be served at Philip's stall. When he saw me smiling, he winked and handed me a package. "For you," he said. "No money . . . every week, come."

My next task was to solve the bread problem. I thought I could make bread myself, but I had no oven. Could I make pita on hot stones like I had seen Arabs do in Egyptian villages? But I had no recipe for Arab bread. A few days later, I met a young Swiss engineer who was in Dodoma to teach Tanzanians to use solar power for cooking instead of charcoal. Tanzania's forests had been decimated over the years, and a reforestation effort had begun. However, Tanzanians were used to cooking with charcoal, and the health of these sparse forests was being threatened.

When I mentioned that I was trying to bake bread, he proposed to make me a solar oven. A few days later, he came over with what looked like a long tube of metal lined with foil and topped with a piece of glass. All I had to do, he explained, was to place the bread on the foil, close the glass oven door, and stick the whole contraption in the sun. Great, I thought, but I didn't have any idea how to make the dough! A couple from Australia lived next door who had once lived in the Outback. I decided to ask Mary, the wife—a suntanned, lined woman of fifty—for a recipe. She complied and threw in a couple of packets of yeast along with a well-worn paperback cookbook detailing the basics of Australian-style bread. Once I mixed all the ingredients, Thomas kneaded it with a vengeance. It not only rose, but nearly exploded out of my wooden bowl. We shaped the dough into two baguettes, stuck them in the tubular oven, and perched it on a flat rock in the sun. Thomas squatted right by it and waited, staring through the glass. It took two hours for those loaves to bake, and they came out dense and a bit chewy, but we had succeeded nonetheless. From that day on, we baked bread once a week. We played around with the recipe, and the loaves improved over time . . . but only slightly.

Every morning Thomas and I took a walk through the town, going from store to store, trying to find things to cook. Indian Sikhs owned most of the shops, as well as ran construction companies and exchanged currency with the expatriate community. These shops were invariably dimly lit and sparsely stocked. You might find aspirin, Pepto-Bismol, makeup, toilet paper, potatoes, and the Tanzanian staple *ugali*. One day, as we entered one of the stores whose owner Jimmy knew quite well, I saw a woman leaving with a basket filled with vegetables. I asked the young Indian woman wearing a summer-weight sari that always stood patiently behind the counter if I, too, could have some fresh vegetables. Selma paused and looked at me with curiosity in her face. "Do you have any makeup to sell?" she asked in a whisper. I remembered all the makeup I had bought in New York. "Yes," I said. "I do." She asked me to bring it to her the next day, assuring me that she'd sell me some vegetables. That night, after I told Jimmy about my encounter, he told me that the Sikhs ran a clandestine bus from Dodoma over the Kenyan border because Nyerere had officially closed the border between Tanzania and Kenya. Tanzania had magnificent game parks, but most tourists went to Kenya, which had a more sophisticated tourist industry. The Kenyans would bring the tourists across the border to access Tanzanian parks and pocket the fees. This clandestine bus was a great moneymaking scheme for the Sikhs, who sold the vegetables they brought back from Kenya at a premium price or in exchange for things the young Indian women could not get in Dodoma. The next day, I brought the list of vegetables I wanted along with a large selection of American drugstore eye makeup and one of my larger baskets. Selma told me to come back in two days to collect my vegetables. Two days later, Selma handed me my basket. It contained vegetables I hadn't asked for, but which I was content with: a cauliflower, overgrown zucchini, and a large head of lettuce. We hadn't had a green salad in nearly a month! Every week from then on, I went back to Selma with eye makeup, blushes, and creams in exchange for more produce. I later befriended Selma and often went to the store to chat with her. She had wanted to be a teacher, but here in Dodoma, her life was very restricted, and the only thing she could do was study by correspondence, which took a long time. "I will have to get married soon," she said. "I am twenty, and my father will find me a husband, and I will not be able to continue to study." Sikh women went to temple in groups and met, once married, at one another's house. I was the first friend that Selma had who was not a Sikh.

A few weeks later, Selma told me that her cousin was getting married; she wondered if I could make something for the dinner her parents were having for the fiancé's family . . . something French, she mused. I thought about the liver Philip was giving me every week. Maybe I could make a liver pâté. It turned out that she had a large charcoal oven at home, so I prepared the ingredients for the pâté, assembled it, and took it to her house. We placed it the oven and prayed for the best. Forty minutes later, the pâté looked as if I had cooked it in my own oven in New York. It was a great success at the pre-wedding dinner, and I was in business. I made two to three pâtés a week in exchange for vegetables and fruit. Bartering had become my way of life.

I made very few friends among the expatriates, who let it be known that they didn't quite approve of my friendships with Tanzanians and Sikhs. They tended to avoid me because I often talked about my new Tanzanian friends and their children. There were a few exceptions, including a couple from Holland who had lived in Dodoma for many years. Margaret, the wife, was an excellent cook and gardener who produced strawberries, spinach, string beans, and radishes and had the best papaya trees in Dodoma. They also had a wonderful garden of local plants and had parrots and even a small monkey. Thomas and I would often visit them for afternoon tea. I think Thomas had a crush on their daughter, Elisabeth, and I loved Margaret's pancakes. Small, thin, and round, they were a cross between a crêpe and an American pancake. She served them with stewed strawberries from her garden. Thomas and I would wolf down at least six at each sitting. She also taught me to have no fear of garden snakes; we had several in our own garden. Her husband, Gustaf, worked for the government. He was a geologist and was teaching the Tanzanians to find and mine Tanzanite, a sparkling diamond-like stone that, when heated, turns a magnificent purple. Another couple I befriended was Jimmy's Habitat boss and his wife. Mr. and Mrs. Kidhane Alamayehu were Ethiopian and had also lived in Dodoma for several years. Mrs. Alamayehu came often to visit, dressed in pale colored gowns with flowing scarves around her shoulders. She cooked well, serving us spicy chopped beef in a red-hot sauce and vegetables in a green, spicy sauce with *injira,* a flat, soft, pancake-like bread prepared with fermented flour. Her table was always beautifully laid out with exotic flowers and silver cutlery. She also prepared some French dishes. She loved hard-boiled eggs in aspic or served with a mayonnaise or French grated carrot salad. We sat on low stools and ate with our hands, using the bread to pick up the meat or the sauce. I often wondered where she got these wonderful ingredients, but her husband was Jimmy's boss, and I never dared ask. Often when she visited me, she would sit and question me about America, New York, and French recipes.

Among the expatriates were Italians, Danes, and a large colony of Chinese who ran the local hospital. They would nod when I'd see them in town, but they never spoke to us. I would meet one of them soon enough, when I was bitten on my heel by an insect. It hurt a lot and quite soon my heel became swollen, and I knew I had to remove the stinger. Thomas and I drove to the Chinese hospital, a white-washed building with benches all around the entrance, teeming with Tanzanians who had some ailment or other, often malaria or the flu, which that much later we learned was not flu but AIDS; the epidemic would soon ravage Tanzania and most of the rest of the continent. Because we were foreigners, we were immediately taken to the Chinese doctor. I explained what had happened as I looked around the dirty, fly-swarmed office. *Would I lose my foot from the sting, or would I lose it from an infection because of the dirt around me?* The doctor seemed to read my mind and said, "Go home, open the wound with a clean, sharp knife, and remove the sting. Wash it with alcohol, and take these pills. Antibiotics."

When we got home, I burned the blade of a Swiss Army knife

and looked at Thomas. Could I really ask Thomas to cut my heel open? Thomas was only twelve, but in the last few months, our relationship had changed. He was today more my friend than my son. I had taken him everywhere with me as he spoke Swahili better than I did and could converse with people. I discussed my plans with him and often asked his advice. At night, as we could not leave him alone in the house, he came with us as we socialized. Also, when we read to one another, the books were those we or he wanted to read. Thomas started to discuss books with us, which he had never done before.

I looked in his large blue-gray eyes and asked, "Can you cut my heel and remove the sting?" Thomas seemed quite confident that he could perform the operation. We poured alcohol on the wound, cut the skin, removed the sting, applied antibiotic ointment and a bandage, and hoped for the best. A few days later my wound was closed.

Another month had gone by, and a routine set in. Jimmy left the house very early in the morning and came home for lunch, then would return to the office while Thomas and I would explore our surroundings. Jimmy would return by five, often with his team. In New York, there had been an almost total separation between Jimmy's office and home. Here in Dodoma, drawings of the new capital were pinned to the wall, and often his associates, tired of eating badly, would come and share our dinner. They discussed the plans or the problems they had with the authorities. Thomas listened and sometimes contributed to the talk because he now knew the city quite well. Thomas had quite a number of Tanzanian friends, was often invited to their houses, and was aware of how they lived.

In the afternoon, while Thomas was away with his friends, I had nothing much to do, so one day I decided that I would write a new cookbook with recipes that I had dreamt of while cooking with whatever I had found in the market. Mainly, I wanted to write a diet book because Jimmy and Thomas had lost weight, but I hadn't. I had stopped smoking and was wolfing down roasted peanuts all day long.

On a large piece of translucent yellow drafting paper, I wrote a list of vegetables that were not available in the Dodoma market, then a list of meats, and another of seafood I knew. I began to mix and match new, simple recipes and wrote them down on an old typewriter I borrowed from Kahama's office. Very soon I had a long list of recipes but had to wait until I went back to New York to test them. A year later, *Colette's Slim Cuisine* came out. The book was illustrated with Jimmy's drawings of city scenes made out of vegetables, meat, fish, and pasta. The press was kind, the public was not. Could you really lose weight with such scrumptious recipes scoffed one of the reviews in the newspaper? One could; I was the living proof. But judging by sales, few believed me.

Back in Dodoma, August was approaching, and so was Jimmy's birthday. *What could Thomas and I give him?* There was little to buy in Dodoma, and the roads to Dar es Salaam were flooded. On one of our walking expeditions, we discovered a local stadium where the Tanzanians played soccer. All around the stadium were small ivory shops selling creamy white ivory bracelets, necklaces, and rings that were laid out on black cloth. I asked one of the merchants if he could make a piece of ivory jewelry if I gave him a design. "No problem," he said. I wasn't convinced, but I decided to take the risk. I asked John Diebboll, Jimmy's young assistant, to secretly give me a sketch of the plan of the new capital, and I asked the ivory dealer to carve the design onto a piece of ivory. "No problem! Come in three days; it will be ready." He told me that it would cost me 100 shillings. I took out my little calculator to see how much it was in dollars. As the man saw it, he said,

"Nothing! You give me the calculator, and I give you the carving."
An incredible deal! My bartering was at its peak. On the day of
Jimmy's birthday, I invited his team and a few of our friends. I
handed Jimmy the carving, wrapped up just as the carver had
given to me, in a piece of rough black cloth. I was as surprised as
Jimmy when he opened it: A large concave piece of ivory was
carved on one side with a perfect outline of the future center of
the capital. He had tears in his eyes when he said, "It is the best
birthday present I ever got!"

Sometimes, Jimmy would give me the keys to his jeep. Thomas
and I would drive from Dodoma into the bush, visiting small Wagogo villages or sometimes Masai encampments. The Masai were
very tall, thin, and always wrapped in magnificent colored cloths
with intricate bead jewelry around their necks and long heavy
earrings dangling that elongated their ears. The women were also
bejeweled; however, their necklaces were larger with more intricate designs. They often had a sleeping baby strapped to their
back. It was hard to speak with them since most of them spoke a
special dialect. The Wagogos, on the contrary, spoke Swahili.
Their houses were very strange. They were rectangular, built of
mud and straw, but they were half sunken into the ground, with
extremely low ceilings. Dried gourds, used as drinking vessels
and cooking pots, hung from the wood-pole rafters. Often the
gourds would be decorated and sold at the market. The houses
were almost bare: a few low stools, a couple of hammocks, and,
in one corner, a circle of large stones—the stove. The Wagogos,
although very poor, always greeted us with warmth and offered
to share with us whatever drink they had. Their land was bare and
difficult to cultivate. There was no industry that could offer some
work. Thomas and I got to know a Wagogo family quite well, and
between the family's broken English and our few words of
Swahili, we managed to learn a lot from this family. Their older

son went to school; his younger brother could not because he had no shoes, and the school would not admit him without shoes. The next day we gathered Thomas's old sneakers for the young Wagogo boy. Later, we visited the school and were appalled. Housed in a crumbling, white washed concrete block building on a small courtyard, the school had very few books and hardly any paper or pencils.

When I went back to New York in the fall, I asked my friends for donations and sent books, boxes of pencils, and shoes to Dodoma, hoping that all the kids in the Wagogo village would be able to go to school.

The following year we returned in the summer to Dodoma. This time I was really prepared. I knew exactly what food to bring: boxes of flour ready to be turned into bread by just adding water; cans of meats, cans of vegetables, and bras of all sizes for bartering, plus clothing for the young Wagogo children and notebooks for the school that I bought in Paris. As this was to be our last summer in Tanzania, Jimmy decided to take us for a long weekend to visit a game park. We flew to Ngorongoro Crater and saw elephants roaming freely, hippopotamus swimming, and hyenas eating while we waited to drive on. On another weekend, Jimmy and Thomas climbed to the top of Tanzania's highest mountain, Kilimanjaro, while I contented myself with climbing with great difficulties to the first stage.

At the end of the summer, the day before we left Dodoma, a stream of Tanzanians came to bid us good-bye. Our new Wagogo friends came too, carrying dark brown wooden stools made of a single piece of wood, carved ivory bracelets, and multicolored cloths. For Thomas, they brought a ceremonial wooden spear.

To this day, I miss Tanzania. I was bitten by the African bug. I loved the country and its people. I had made many friends, and from afar, followed their lives, hoping that one day I would return.

In September, back in New York for the beginning of the school year, I was restless. Once again, I found myself scheming to travel to some faraway country. This time I put all my effort to find a way to go to Japan. Japanese restaurants were opening everywhere in New York, and I wanted to learn more about their cuisine.

At my friend Arakawa's suggestion, I joined the Japan Society and met Peter Grilli, who was their culture and movie director. Peter was short and woolly like a lovable teddy bear. He had been brought up in Japan, where his father was a well-known music critic. He loved Japan and Japanese culture and cuisine. He very quickly understood my curiosity for Japanese ingredients and ways of preparing food, as I often dragged him to Japanese restaurants asking hundreds of questions. Very quickly I learned that Japanese food wasn't merely sushi and sashimi, which had started to sweep New York City, but was an incredibly complex and fascinating cuisine. Peter taught me how to order and ask for dishes that were not on the menu, such as soba, the buckwheat noodle, eaten cold with a dipping sauce; tiny broiled sardines; or sautéed eggplant topped with bonito shavings that seemed to be alive, moving in the air.

One day, Peter announced that he was organizing a gastronomic tour of Japan for the Japan Society's most important supporters and trustees. I was envious, but the trip was very expensive, and I simply could not afford it. A month before they were to leave for Japan, Peter approached me. Would I like to join the group? He needed someone who had some knowledge of Japanese food, someone who would ask intelligent questions and discuss food with the chefs who were going to prepare very special meals. We would be traveling in Japan for three weeks. The only thing that I had to do was to make a small contribution to the Japan Society. The trip was in June, so I would be finished with teaching. But what about my four children? I was hoping that Jimmy would accept my going and take care of the kids. My friend Elisabeth once again came to the rescue. The children could come and join her children in East Hampton, and Lucy would go with them. Jimmy very reluctantly accepted my departure.

"I will miss you, but I left you when I went to Tanzania," he said with a sad smile, "so now it is your turn, and three weeks is not that long."

On the plane to Tokyo, I learned that most of my companions were going to Japan mainly to buy antiques. No one, it seemed, was too excited about the gastronomic tour, and I understood why Peter had asked me to join them.

On our first evening in Tokyo, Peter announced that we were invited by the emperor's principal chef for a kaiseki dinner. A kaiseki dinner, Peter explained, is based on food of the season and also on the chef's mood and inspiration. The dinner proceeds through a series of small dishes, each one a work of art as the dish itself is an important part of the presentation. There is harmony in the order of the dishes, their color, texture, and taste. Just before dinner, he added, the emperor's chef would demonstrate how he prepares a fish that later would be served to us as tempura.

That night, we sat on brocade cushions in a large tatami room of a low building attached to the emperor's palace. In front of us was a low stage fitted with a dark lacquer table where, I assumed, the chef would prepare the fish. When the chef entered the room, there was a murmur of astonishment from all of us. The chef looked like a priest or a great lord in one of Kurasawa's epic films. He wore a black, shiny silk hat tied around his chin and a white, billowing robe with a magnificent gold-threaded rope around his waist. As he crouched in front of the table set in the center of the stage, two young servants, dressed in black, brought in a silver platter with a large black fish set on seaweed. The chef picked up a long silver chopstick with one hand and a long thin knife with the other and proceeded to filet the fish, never touching it with his hands. I looked at the chef, mesmerized, in awe of his dexterity. *How did he do it?* The knife seemed to fly from one side of the fish to the other. Like magic, within ten minutes, four clean filets were set on the silver platter.

Later we were led to a dining room. There, a low table was laid with twenty black lacquered trays decorated with gold bamboo leaves. Thin slices of a very pale tuna were arranged in the shape of a flower. Near the fish was a small, green glass bowl filled with soy sauce. As we sat down on silk damask cushions, we were offered small sake cups, each different, each more beautiful than the next. I chose a pale, white translucent china cup. Into the cups very dry sake was poured by beautiful, kimono-clad young women.

Slowly the dinner unfolded, one dish after another, each more exquisite than the last. One dish that I will never forget was the tempura fish. Our black trays were removed, replaced by a pure white translucent trays, reminiscent of the chef's white robe. On each tray was a square of bamboo in the shape of the table on which the fish had been cut. The bamboo was surrounded with fresh bamboo leaves. Fish filets of golden tempura were strung on carved wood skewers and set on top of the leaves. Near each was a snowy white mountain of finely grated white radish. A black lacquered bowl with half a gold moon painted on its side was filled with a transparent dipping sauce. It was so amazingly beautiful that I hesitated for a moment to pick up the tiny morsels of fried fish. The tempura fish was crunchy, light, and not oily. Twelve small dishes followed, each intricately prepared, each in its own setting. For dessert we were served a pink-tinted ball on an ice-carved plate. Called Cherry Blossom Mochi, it was a sweet glutinous rice ball stuffed with a red-bean paste and rolled in edible brined cherry leaves. The strange combination of bland soft rice and the overly sweet bean with a lemony aftertaste made the perfect finale to a spectacular meal.

The next day, we drove about two hours south of Tokyo to a *ryokan,* a traditional Japanese inn, set on the edge of the sea. That night Peter explained to me that near the ocean at the bottom of the hill was a superb *onsen,* a Japanese bath overlooking the sea. If I went very early, say five o'clock in the morning, he explained, I would be alone. Experiencing a Japanese bath was worth getting up at the crack of dawn. So the next morning, dressed in my kimono and with flip-flop slippers, I went down three flights of wooden stairs to the building that housed the bath. A very old man greeted me at the door and with gestures explained that I should undress and place my clothes in the basket he was handing me. I did as he requested, feeling a bit embarrassed to be nude in front of this old man, but he did not seem to look or care. He then led me to a room surrounded with glass walls. In the center was a very large pool of hot clean water. Along the walls were faucets and low wooden stools. The old man gestured toward the faucets. I understood that I had to wash myself first, then rinse the soap off, and then go in the water. I did what he motioned me to do and then slowly slid into the very hot water. As I stood crouching in the water, I looked at the sun slowly rising over the horizon. Its golden rays were playing with the calm surface of the water. I was lost in my dreams. I felt so in tune with my surroundings, that I thought that perhaps in one of my former lives I had been born a Japanese noblewoman. The hot water was so relaxing, my surroundings so extraordinary that I forgot the time. Suddenly, I realized that I was no longer alone in the pool. As I glanced discreetly behind me, I saw four men in the pool looking my way. In panic I wondered, *What should I do? Should I get up, climb the few steps, and cross the length of the pool nude?* I decided against it and felt that I could wait. These men would not be here forever. When they left, I would get up. Half an hour went by. The skin of my hands was all crinkled by the heat and water, but the men were still there. I knew I could not stay in the water any longer, so I decided to get up, climb the few steps, and walk across the length of the pool, reasoning that I did not know these men and probably would never see them again. So without looking, I did just that, feeling their eyes on me as I went back to the old man to pick up my clothes. At breakfast that morning, I told Peter the story just as the same four men entered the dining room and were introduced to us as the owners of the *ryokan*. The men smiled but said nothing; I looked the other way while Peter laughed at my embarrassment, whispering that I had made their day, and he was sure I would be sent flowers. To my total embarrassment, they did just that!

For the next two weeks, we traveled through Japan. We went north to the temple of Issey, and we had dinner in the headpriest's private dining room, feasting on food I never had eaten before while facing a most extraordinary Zen garden of sand and rocks, so incredibly peaceful. Then we went on to a Buddhist temple where we were served a vegetarian dinner that defied the imagination. What we thought was steak were mushrooms, and what we thought was fish were vegetables.

Our next stop was Osaka to visit the famous French-Japanese cooking school and visit the Bunraku Theater. Later we flew to Kanazawa on the west coast of Japan. Kanazawa was and is the center of lacquer. We went to visit a very great lacquer artist, one of the "living treasures" of Japan. Visiting his house was like visiting the inner sanctum of a lacquer museum. There was intricately designed furniture, vases, bowls, and Geisha combs of all sizes. As we left, we each were handed a small box hiding a lovely black and gold lacquer bowl.

The next day we left for Wajima, a small fishing village on the end of a peninsula. It was home to hundreds of types of seaweed drying in the sun. All along the harbor where the fishermen brought their catch and the divers their seaweed was an extraordinary, mile-long vegetable, fish, and seaweed market. The women in Wajima, I was told, ran the market. There were stands of long strings of dull-looking seaweed next to piles of shimmering seaweed that I remembered eating in salad. But it was the fish that attracted my attention. There were so many different kinds of fish I had never seen before: small and large sardines, mountains of miniscule fish that once dried would be served on top of rice next to, what looked to me, a young tuna, and near it, whale blubber that I was told, was a great delicacy for the Japanese. After the fish market stands, the vegetable stands followed with every color and shape of eggplants, vats of miso filled with cucumbers, carrots, and beans that ended up on our table as pickles.

In the next few days, we flew to Nara and were guests of the Shogun of Nara, who offered us dinner in his ancestral home. In a long, pale green room with sliding shoji screens framed in blond wood were twenty small tables. On the wall was a magnificent calligraphy by a twelfth-century artist. In a corner, a large pale blue iris in a slender bamboo vase with silver filigree stood majestically alone. Across the room, two musicians were playing on ancient violins. As we sat down on low stools, young Japanese kimono-clad waitresses brought out dishes, sliding gracefully to the melancholic music of the musicians. The dinner was like a dream.

Our next stop was Kyoto. I loved Kyoto, with its temples and gardens, but most of all, I loved the indoor market. The market was a mile long, winding around city blocks and selling everything from Kyoto's famed vegetable pickles, the best bean curd I had ever had, transparent, light as air, to embroidered silk kimonos to splendid lacquer ware. While my companions were roaming the antique stores of Kyoto, I spent every minute in the market. On Sunday, I sped to the temple garden where the best flea market in Kyoto was held. I learned to bargain and bought what is today my most precious possession: an iron tea kettle from the eighteenth century.

I often called home and talked to Jimmy and the children. Jimmy was complaining. He was lonely; the children missed me. When was I coming back? Soon, I said, wishing that I could continue to travel and explore Japan. But we had been traveling for two weeks. After Kyoto we were flying back to Tokyo, and to my chagrin, the trip would then be over.

I had a friend in Tokyo. Andre J. was the cultural attaché at the French embassy. A well-known writer, he had been sent to represent French artists in Japan. I had written him that I was coming to Japan, and he invited me to stay with him and his wife until the date of my departure. On our arrival in Tokyo, I was met at the hotel by Andre's housekeeper, Eufemia, a young Filipino woman. She was to take me to Andre's home. On the way she told me the most astonishing news: Andre's wife had run away with the Greek cultural attaché! It was a terrible scandal in Tokyo; Andre was crushed. The French Ambassador was embarrassed by the scandal. The situation, Eufemia said, was a mess.

What was I doing here I asked myself? But my ticket home was not for another three days. I knew no one in Tokyo; Peter had already left for New York. I had no choice but to stay with Andre.

That night, a devastated Andre told me the story and begged me to stay until the end of the month. As cultural attaché, he had to entertain distinguished guests. He needed me. "Please stay, Colette," he said, with tears in his eyes, "I will pay for your ticket back to New York. I need you." How could I say no? I called Jimmy in New York and begged forgiveness. I had to stay two more weeks in Japan and help Andre cope with the situation. Jimmy was crushed and argued with me for at least ten minutes, and then with a sigh, he gave in saying no more than two weeks.

The next day, as Andre left for the Embassy, I sat down with Eufemia and studied Andre's calendar. He had five dinner parties scheduled for the next two weeks. I asked Eufemia, "What about the menus?"

The cook was also a Filipino. When I studied the menus for these dinners, I thought they were boring, not festive enough. In these special circumstances, we had to offer our guests more exciting fare. Eufemia, who was a very bright, lovely young woman, suggested that she and I go food shopping. And so together (Eufemia spoke Japanese), we went to the wholesale fish market where I bought tiny little crabs, the size of a quarter; cod fish liver that I would sauté like foie gras and serve on a bed of greens. At the vegetable market, I bought burdock that looked like French *salsifi,* fresh shiitake mushrooms, and Japanese persimmons to make a mousse for dessert. The cook and I prepared the first dinner. We sautéed the crabs and served them as appetizers with the drinks. Then the cook made a clear soup, adding at the last minute some seaweed I had brought from Wajima. As a main course, I stuffed thin slices of chicken breast with fresh shiitake mushrooms and sliced garlic and surrounded it with a sauce made with the Japanese Uzu lemon. Tiny potatoes sautéed with rosemary finished the dish. The dessert was a mousse of Japanese persimmons. The dinner was a success, and Andre seemed to be calmer.

A few days later, Andre announced that among our next guests were the owners of Seibu, the largest department store in Tokyo with a very important art museum attached to it. Andre had been planning an important show of French painters and was afraid that the Seibu owners might cancel the show. I promised I would make a very special dinner. On my walks through the Tokyo vegetable market, I had discovered that Japanese cucumbers were very long, narrow, and had very few seeds. I decided that the appetizer would be small chunks of cucumber like miniature wells, filled with salmon caviar entwined with edible greens and topped with crème fraîche. They were to be set on *shiso* leaves, surrounded with vegetable pickles from Kyoto in light aspic. The next course was to be a soup of Adzuki beans with endives followed by a poached fresh salmon served with pomegranate and *nashi,* a Japanese pear-apple that is today common in the United States but that I had never eaten before. With it I served grated mountain potato mixed with thinly sliced cooked okra and a parsley sauce. For dessert I tried something that I was terrified would not work, a mousse of fresh bean curd with imported raspberries. That night the owner of Seibu arrived dressed in traditional ancient Japanese clothing—the most beautiful kimono I had ever seen, made of silk and silver threads. He was followed by his slender, pale, stunning Japanese wife, who was dressed in a brocaded kimono of gold and silver threads. The dinner went very well. Our Seibu guests smiled and complimented me on the dinner. By making a slightly strange dinner, I was afraid that I had ruined Andre's chance for a museum show.

The next day I received an invitation from Kodansha International, a large publishing house. To my astonishment, they wanted to talk to me about a cookbook. At the meeting, it transpired that our guests of the previous night had raved about the dinner I had served and felt that the Japanese would enjoy a cookbook that used Japanese ingredients in such an original way.

I was very flattered, but I told the publisher, "Although I love Japanese food, I cannot cook like a Japanese. Japanese cooking requires years of training and hours of preparation. I work in New York, and I have no time to spend hours in the kitchen. What I like to do is cook Japanese ingredients my way but serve them in the spirit of Japanese cooking tradition. I will give them recipes different from what they are used to." For the next two weeks, we discussed a book contract. Finally, it was decided that I was to come back to Japan at their expense and explore other Japanese cooking traditions. I thought, just for a minute, that my family and Jimmy would not like that, but I said yes very quickly.

I left Andre though he was still worried about his future. Later, I was pleased to learn that Seibu happily gave him permission to use their gallery to show the work of French painters. The dinner had worked! However, a few months later, he was recalled to Paris and resumed his career as a writer.

Back in New York, I prepared myself for another trip to Japan, talking to Arakawa, Peter Grilli, and other Japanese friends to plan my itinerary the following June. I made a list of cities that I wanted to visit.

The following June, I left, once again for Tokyo. On my arrival, I was visited by Hiroshi Teshigahara, the filmmaker I had met at the Arakawas. I had loved his film, *Woman in the Dunes*. Hiroshi was also a master of flower arrangement and had a very successful school teaching young women classical Japanese flower arrangement. A few days after I arrived in Tokyo, Hiroshi asked me if I would do a friend of his a great favor. The friend had invested in several *crêperies,* but the business was failing, and he wanted me to look at the restaurants to see why they were such a failure. For the next two days, I visited the *crêperies* and realized immediately that the batter was wrong and that the cooks had not leaned how to make a perfect crêpe. I gathered all the cooks together in one of the restaurants, made a batter, and taught them how to make a real French crêpe.

The next day the owner sent his manager to the hotel where I was staying. He handed me an envelope and said, bowing very low, "Please count the money. Mr. O. is so pleased and thankful for your help." I refused the envelope, saying "I did very little. Thank you, but there is no need." He insisted, and so I opened the envelope and nearly had a heart attack as I counted the money. There was the equivalent of $30,000 in my trembling hands. Bowing even lower, I thanked them both and rushed to my room. I picked up the phone, called Jimmy, waking him up, and told him to take the first plane to Tokyo to join me, explaining briefly what had happened.

A few days later, Jimmy arrived, and together we traveled, eating our way through Tokyo, Kyoto, and Osaka. Jimmy took pictures, and I took notes of everyone and every dish we ate.

A year later, Jimmy told me that his firm was doing very well. "Thomas is graduating this spring. He will be going to college in the fall. We can manage without your teaching. Would you like to quit school and just write?"

This had been my dream for several years, and so the following June, I resigned from my position at school and said good-bye to all my friends. I shed a tear or two, and with great trepidation and fear, I looked forward to a year of not only just writing, but also traveling and this time writing about it.

⤜⤛

CHICKEN LIVER MOUSSE

Clean 1 pint of fresh chicken livers, removing fat and gristle. In a large skillet, melt 2 tablespoons of butter and sauté the livers for 3 minutes on each side. Sprinkle with salt and pepper and 1 tablespoon of dry tarragon. Remove the livers and place in a food processor along with 2 eggs and 1 cup of heavy cream. Process until all the ingredients are pureed. Strain the mixture through a fine sieve. Pour the strained and pureed livers into a 2-quart soufflé dish. Place the soufflé dish in a baking pan and add 6 cups of water to the pan to create a water bath. Bake in a 350° oven for 40 minutes. Remove from the oven and cool. Refrigerate until ready to serve. Serve with toasted baguettes.

Serves 4.

LONG CHINESE STRING BEANS

For this dish you need 1 pound of string beans; cut each string beans in four pieces. Place in a saucepan and cover with boiling water and 1 teaspoon of salt. Bring to a boil, reduce the heat, and cook for 8 minutes. Drain. In the same saucepan, melt 2 tablespoons of butter. Add 2 minced garlic cloves, ½ cup of chopped parsley, and salt and pepper. Cook for 3 minutes, stirring all the while, then add the string beans, mix well, and simmer for 4 minutes. Serve with roast chicken or steak.

DIPPING SAUCE FOR RAW VEGETABLES

In a food processor, place 1 cup of spinach, stems removed, with 1 cup of watercress, stems removed; 2 cups of plain yogurt; the juice of half a lemon; and 2 tablespoons of olive oil. Process until all the ingredients are pureed. Remove to a bowl, add salt and pepper to taste, and refrigerate until ready to serve.

Makes 3 cups.

Standing in front of our Sullivan Street house

7

The Journalist

❧❧

Every few years Jimmy would give me a wonderful present for my birthday: a bound book written and illustrated by him. Each of the books told the story of what had happened to me in the last few years or decade, picking up where he had left off before. Today, as I sat down to write, I picked up the 1979 to 1989 book and looked at his magnificent drawings. I flipped through the book and saw a drawing of me topless in an open bath house in Japan; a drawing of my daughter Marianne being married in our garden; a drawing of me writing in a tiny room surrounded by hundreds of cookbooks.

By the fall of 1988, I had stopped teaching at St. Ann's in order to devote myself full-time to writing. The first few weeks were difficult. I had to adjust to the fact that I did not have to get up at six in the morning to be at school at 8:30 A.M., that there were no children to take care of. Marianne was about to get married and dreaming about becoming a teacher, Juliette was in Turkey teaching English to young girls, and Cecile was about to embark on an architectural career. As for Thomas, Jimmy and I had just driven him, our youngest child, to Dartmouth College. Now during the day, the house was empty. I was free to do whatever I wanted. I did nothing for a few weeks; I roamed around the house aimlessly, thinking over and over, *What if I could not find anything to do? What if I have no ideas for stories? What if people forget me? What if the telephone never rings?* I was scared and lonely and missed the challenge of teaching and the conversation and laughter of my teacher friends. I missed the anticipation of creating new programs. I missed running my department.

To prepare for my "new life" as a full-time writer, I began by organizing my space in the house. Until now, I had used the smallest room in the house as my study. I decided to move my books and computer to one of the children's deserted bedrooms. The room was large and airy, and I hated it. I missed the comfort of my compact office, and so I moved back. I tried to work but failed to write even a single line. I was experiencing not only the "empty nest" syndrome, but also a change in the way I looked not only at my work but also at my life. For years I had taught because we needed the money. What I had really wanted to do was pushed aside simply out of necessity. But when the opportunity came my way, I had to cope with too much change all at once. The same month I resigned from St. Ann's, I lost my job at *New York* Magazine.

New York Magazine had been my lifeline to the food world. Years before, I had started to write short pieces for their "Best Bets" section. It all started when I met Gael Greene, the food edi-

tor of *New York* magazine at a party in East Hampton. We had a lot
in common. We both liked good food, we were both good cooks,
and, above all, we both liked to write about it.

One day I received a call from Gael. Would I be interested in
becoming The Underground Gourmet restaurant reviewer for
New York magazine? I had wanted to review restaurants for many
years, and this, I thought, would be the perfect job for me. Gael
explained that the magazine was considering three other writers
for this spot. The rules of the underground gourmet column
were very strict. No main dish could cost more than $8.50, not
an easy criterion to meet even in 1982. But I knew Chinatown
and ethnic restaurants very well, so I was sure I could do the job.
Gael suggested that I choose a restaurant and write a review.

I chose an Ethiopian restaurant on Thompson Street. I had two
very close Ethiopian friends, and had eaten at their house several
times. Also, I was introduced to Ethiopian food on my visits to
Africa. I felt I knew the food quite well. So I wrote my piece, had
Jimmy check for English and grammar mistakes, and sent it in. A
few weeks later, I was hired.

I worked as The Underground Gourmet reviewer for the next
three years. I loved discovering small, new restaurants. I remember once walking to visit South Street Seaport, which had just
opened. I had lost my way and ended up on a side street. I noticed a seafood restaurant that advertised mussels, a whole bowl
with Italian bread for only $6. The restaurant was empty, the
mussels were deliciously fresh, and when I spoke to the owner, I
was astonished to learn that he was a wholesale fish monger at
the Fulton Fish Market. He had always dreamt of opening a
restaurant. He was trying to make a go at it, but had not been
quite successful. I wrote the story, and a few weeks later, passing
by I saw a line of customers waiting to be seated. Another discovery was a bistro called La Luncheonette, on Essex Street, run by

a Frenchmen who was the cook, the waiter, and the sommelier. A year after my story was published, he moved his restaurant to Tenth Avenue and was able to hire a waiter and a dishwasher. Success stories made me very proud.

Every year, apart from restaurant reviews, I worked on the *Round up of New Restaurants* issue; stories on the best potato pancake in New York, the best barbeque, the best restaurants for take out, and many more. Writing these survey stories was incredibly hard work. My writing was straightforward, very accurate and knowledgeable in describing the food or the décor, but I knew that my style did not quite match the witty, trendy *New York* magazine "new journalism" style. This would prove my downfall.

In 1988, Chinatown saw an explosion of new restaurants. Loaded with cash, Chinese were arriving in droves from Hong Kong. They were used to much better fare than the mushy meals served in New York's traditional Chinese restaurants, which were geared to an imagined American taste. I suggested a piece on the best new restaurants in Chinatown. My piece would describe the many dishes new to New York. Everyone at the magazine agreed that this was a great idea, and I set out to select the ten best. I turned to my closest Chinese friend, Suzanne Chen. Suzanne and I ate our way through Chinatown. I wrote my piece and presented my expense account. The editor-in-chief liked my story but said that it lacked the *New York* magazine voice. Furthermore, he added, he was astonished by my soaring expenses. "Look," he said, brandishing my expense account, "you say here that a bird's nest soup cost $30! That's outrageous!" He then pulled out of his desk drawer a soiled take-out menu from the hole-in-the wall Chinese restaurant around the corner. "Look, a perfectly good bird's nest soup here is only five bucks. I'll pay you for the article but will not reimburse your expense account. Take it or leave it!"

I tried to explain that the bird's nest soup I had written about was the real thing. What he ate at his desk was just make believe, a tasteless version. Refusing to back down, I walked out and thus lost a job I had loved more than any other.

So now I was a freelance journalist. It is a very difficult job, no matter how well-known you may be. I was not shy, but I found it very tough to knock on doors, and also at this point, I had no idea of what I wanted to write. A chance encounter put me in the right direction.

The food world was changing dramatically. The Greenmarket on Union Square, a Farmers' Market thought up by our friend Barry Benepe, was now offering chefs' ingredients available formerly only from Europe or Asia that local farmers were now growing on New York and New Jersey farms near the city. In the Greenmarket on Union Square and in the new Korean produce stores, herbs such as fresh pineapple mint, real French tarragon, purple basil, or Greek oregano, and organic vegetables were becoming ordinary, daily fare. New Yorkers were now clamoring for better breads. Bakeries such as Our Daily Bread and the Sullivan Street Bakery were opening in many neighborhoods in New York, offering French baguettes, croissants, or Italian *cibatta* or *Pugliese*. Dean & Deluca, Balducci's, Whole Foods, and Gourmet Garage in the Village were a few of the pioneering stores where one shopped for unique ingredients from the world over.

Soho had greatly changed since we had bought our house in 1967. Up Sullivan Street from our house. Once Upon A Tart, the gourmet café run by Jerome, served small vegetarian quiches, scrumptious sandwiches, and exotic salads along with excellent muffins, cheddar-dill scones (I was addicted to them), fruit tarts, and rich black French roast coffee. Around the corner on Prince Street, Luigi's restaurant was replaced by Raoul's, a hot French restaurant, filled with beautiful people. It had just received a two-star rating from *The New York Times*. There were many new trendy boutiques such as Diesel Jeans, Hans Koch leather bags, and a Tibetan silk and jewelry store, and, most important, a twenty-four-hour Korean vegetable grocery with a street-side flower shop at the corner of Thompson and Prince Streets, which changed the whole aspect of the street. But my favorite place was Dean & Deluca, a brilliant new grocery and produce store on Prince Street and Broadway. The store was the idea of two men, Joel Dean, who took care of the buying, and Jack Ceglic, who designed the store. Added to this pair, was a third man, an Italian, Georgio Deluca, whose main interest was cheeses from all over the world.

One day walking down Prince Street, I stopped short in front of Dean & Deluca's window. I could not believe my eyes. The window looked like a window from Fauchon's in Paris. Intrigued, I entered the store and asked Joel Dean who had designed the window. Joel introduced me to Lee Grimsbo. Lee was a tall, young, laconic man with a shy smile. He came from the Midwest and was the son of a biologist who got Lee interested in the cultivation of organic fruit and vegetables. What Lee wanted most in life, he told me, was to share his knowledge with the public and at the same time help his friends. I liked Lee; we had the same goals. Every day I would stop by the store and talk to him, asking about what new vegetable or fruit he had. He brought in cardoons that the Italians had eaten for centuries; he showed me a Romanesco cauliflower from Holland, a cross between a cauliflower and broccoli. I would go to my kitchen, try these new vegetables, and come back to him with recipes I thought he could share with his customers.

One day Lee asked me why I had not written a story about the revolution in the agricultural world in the United States. He suggested a trip around the country where he would introduce me to all his friends. I asked an old friend, Philip Herrera, then managing editor of *Connoisseur* magazine, if he was interested in such a piece. Philip talked to Tom Hoving, editor-in-chief, and my story got the go-ahead. They were willing to pay for the trip.

In early June, Lee and I flew to San Francisco where we visited several of Lee's farmer friends. Most of them were in their twenties, did not come from farming families, and had degrees in English literature, chemistry, engineering, etc. Bored with the prospect of futures as engineers and scientists, they had decided to buy a few acres and start farming. A few told me that Alice Waters of Chez Panisse Restaurant had inspired them to grow vegetables such as ramps, the wild onion, or fiddleheads from the banks of brooks. Some began to grow delicate miniature vegetables. Others visited Europe and came back with seeds for patty pan squash, miniature zucchini, and five different kinds of potatoes; one or two brought back purple potatoes from Peru. We met with very different growers from the Driscoll Company, a large corporate enterprise who caught on to the exotic vegetable and berry market and now grew different kinds of fruit plus salads such as frisee, red leaf, radicchio, and red and white radishes.

We then drove to the Napa Valley, not to look at wineries, but to visit the exquisite Fetzer Winery vegetable garden, precisely planted with Jerusalem artichokes, oriental eggplants, baby leaf spinach, chayotes, tiny Italian artichokes and green or yellow miniature zucchini. On a commune in Sonoma Valley, we hung out with young hippies who cultivated, in a very large garden, white asparagus, fennel, and five kinds of lettuce they called *mesclun,* and they sold these at nearby farmer's markets. As we walked through the commune garden, wilder looking than the others we had visited, Lee picked up a tiny purple salad leaf: "Look Colette how small and delicate! It belongs to the spinach family. Taste it; it's so amazingly sweet."

As he handed me the delicate pale green leaf, he looked happier than I had ever seen him appear in New York. I thought that this was where he belonged, not in the cutthroat New York food scene.

Later that day we drove to the Oakland Museum, which one weekend a year hosted farmers from around the state, inviting them to display new varieties of vegetables and fruit. We met Nicolas T., a Californian who grew *nishi* or Asian pears and *mizuma* salad that he had first tasted in Japan. Another stand was displaying red, yellow, and orange Tom Thumb tomatoes, even smaller than cherry tomatoes, which were grown on a miniscule farm near Oakland.

Then we flew to Los Angeles to meet Frieda, the "purple lady" (she was always dressed in purple), who was wildly successful, packaged container loads of vegetables like tomatillos and baby avocados and fruit like feijoa or carambola, the yellow star fruit from South America and the Caribbean Islands, and shipped her products to thousands of gourmet stores around the country.

Finally, just before leaving California, we drove to the famous Chino Farm outside San Diego. The Chino Farm grew superb vegetables and fruit for chefs around the area. The Chino vegetables, herbs, and especially strawberries were mouthwatering, the equal of the best of France. Buyers drove miles to pick up a carton of strawberries, tiny artichokes, or pencil-thin haricot vert.

While in California, we dined at Jeremiah Tower's and Wolfgang Puck's new restaurants whose menus starred all these new vegetables now available in all the farmer's markets.

Back in New York, Lee and I drove to visit farms that grew small zucchini with their flowers still attached, miniature patty pans, and white and purple beets that they would sell at the Greenmarket. We visited Chinese farms to see the two-foot long string beans, the purple and green spinach, and the sweet potato leaves that they grew for Chinese restaurants but increasingly also for chefs of American Nouvelle Cuisine.

Our next trip was to Florida, which now, because of Cuban and South American immigrants, had become an innovative agricultural center. Growers introduced clementines, the small tangerine from Spain and Morocco; star fruit, mangoes which were becoming very popular; several kinds of Mexican peppers: jicama, taro, and mameys, a sweet pear like fruit; and miniature sweet white corn that chefs around the country were using to garnish their dishes.

My piece became the cover story of *Connoisseur,* and I was delighted by the accompanying photographs that made the vegetables look like precious jewels. The success of the story led to other plumb assignments. I wrote about the new farmer's markets that had sprung up all over the country, and I did another story for *Connoisseur* on the century old Baltimore Lexington Market. For *Metropolitan Home,* I wrote on San Miguel de Allende in Mexico and about Chinatown's nouvelle cuisine for *Elle* magazine.

Later, I worked for two years for *McCall's* magazine as their food and design editor. Working for a magazine as an editor was a new experience and very exciting. This led to being asked to create a new magazine aimed at the Midwest. Like almost all new ventures in the publishing world, this was short-lived. Once again I turned to freelance work, never really finding a niche that made me happy.

My oldest daughter Marianne, expecting her first child, was searching for something to do. She suggested that together we could write a vegetable cookbook. It would be a dialogue between mother and daughter. So began a close collaboration between Marianne and me. Together we traveled to farmer's markets; invented recipes, hired a photographer, Greg Sclight, and did the food styling ourselves. The book, *Vegetables,* was published in 1991. It was wild and fun, Craig Claiborne loved it, and so did the rest of the food press. We traveled around the country together as a mother and daughter team. We appeared together on TV and radio.

But Marianne wanted to go back to school, and so our collaboration ended. I felt restless, nervous, and even bored. *What was happening to me?* I was always on the go. Most of the time, I wanted to get out of the house. In reality, I wanted to leave Jimmy for a little while. I needed to get away. I loved him, but I could not stand hearing every night about his office problems and his money worries. Jimmy needed to think about his own future. Architecture, planning cities, or painting? Which one to choose? I thought that, if I went away, he could manage better and see his future more clearly.

One day I read a short article in one of the French magazines I subscribed to. The story was about an Australian who had saved a group of camels roaming the desert of Australia. Apparently in the 1990s, the Australian government had the camels brought in from Afghanistan so that a surveying party could be sent out to map the vast desert. Once the mapping was done, the camels were abandoned. They multiplied and multiplied. The government was about to exterminate the camels as a nuisance when Peter S. decided to save some of them. He went to Afghanistan to learn all about camels. Now, it seemed, he was trying to start a tourist camel-trekking expedition through the desert. His idea was that trekkers would ride across the desert on camels, visit watering holes and Aborigine villages. This sounded very exciting and an answer to my problems. I thought I should pursue the story.

I called the travel editor of *The New York Times* and suggested a story idea: a middle-aged woman on a camel trek across the desert of Australia. She agreed, and for the next three weeks, I planned the trip.

I visited the Australian Tourist bureau, talked with their representative, and made an itinerary that would take me to Cairns in the north to Alice Springs where I would meet the young man and go on a camel trek, then go on to Sydney and Melbourne.

Cairns surprised me. It was an ugly town except for two resort hotels. Cairns was where tourists came to explore Australia's magnificent Barrier Reef. As I had to wait for my contact from the Ministry of Tourism, I decided to go snorkeling like any other tourist. It took me a whole morning to learn how to breathe underwater, but the snorkeling was incredible. Anemones of all colors, incredible living corals, and fish of different sizes and patterns, colors, shapes that blew my mind. The whole adventure was exhilarating.

A day or two later, I was still waiting for my official contact. I walked through the town, which had little to offer a tourist beyond the Great Barrier Reef. No bookstores, no boutiques, and only XXX rated movies. By the second day, I was bored out my mind. When finally my contact arrived, I learned to my utter dismay that the Australian domestic airline was on strike and that we would have to wait another few days.

Finally, three days later we flew off for Alice Springs.

Alice Springs is located in the heart of the Australian desert. It is the home of the famous Ayers Rock, or the *Uluru* in the Aborigines' language. Ayers Rock is an enormous pinkish gray monolith that dominates thirty-six other domed rocks. These rocks are a very important part of the Aborigines' religious beliefs. I wanted to visit the Ayers Rock, but after a quick look, I had to leave for the camel ranch. Because of the strike, we had lost too many days in Cairns.

Peter S., the young camel trainer, had built a very primitive ranch in the desert. The ranch had a few bedrooms with crude showers, a bar, and a simple restaurant for the locals.

I looked for Peter in the bar, which was filled with men in blue jeans and boots drinking beer. As I looked around, a man of about thirty-five, tall, blond, wearing heavy boots, approached me and asked what I wanted.

"I am here to meet someone called Peter S."

"I'm Peter."

Staring at me, a short, middle-aged lady, he suddenly blurted out: "I was really expecting a young woman."

I did not know how to answer, but said, "Don't worry. I grew up in Egypt; I know all about camels."

Relieved, Peter explained that he had expected me a week ago, but that every thing was ready, and we could leave at dawn the next morning. We were going to travel on camels for five days, ending up in an Aborigine village where the head of the council had agreed to house me for a night. During the camel trek, we would sleep in the open air and wash and swim in water holes. Peter would do the cooking.

That morning I followed Peter to the Camel Corral. Peter brought out five camels: one for me; one for him; and one for a helper, who he introduced as John, no last name. John was a scrawny fellow with long, dirty blond sideburns. The two other camels were going to be laden with sleeping bags, cooking utensils, and food and water for the next four days.

Once on the camel's back, I realized that in Egypt I had really never traveled very far. Faced with five uncomfortable hours on a camel's back, I regretted my boast. The camels followed one another in a single file. There was really no good way to talk. This would be a silent trip. I looked around me. The sand was the color of ochre. From time to time, I saw a colorful bird flying away as we approached. The flora and the fauna were very different than in France, or the United States, or East Africa. There were some Acacia trees, smaller than the ones I knew at home; there were also eucalyptus trees, whose smell reminded me of our Cairo garden.

At noon, Peter halted the camels and announced that it was time for lunch. I was relieved as I had to go to the bathroom. Where does one go in the desert? I had not thought of that. I looked around: nothing, not even a tree to hide behind.

"Peter, I need to go to the bathroom."

"To the bathroom? Oh, you mean you have to pee. Go straight ahead; we will look the other way."

And so I had my first experience of public facilities in the Australian desert.

Lunch was ham sandwiches drowned with the local beer. Slightly tipsy, I went back on my camel for another five-hour ride. The sun had come out; the color of the sand was changing. I saw wild flowers that I hadn't noticed before, red flowers with dark black centers, pink ones with white edges, and a strange spiky plant that Peter told me later would bloom after the first rain.

During those five hours, I daydreamed. I thought of work, home, my children, and Jimmy. I felt totally at peace with myself and very content.

When we finally stopped riding, Peter and John made a fire and cooked. They broiled some steaks, made bread, and served some salad. For dessert, we had fruit and cookies. We drank lots of beer, sang songs, and told stories. They asked about New York, my family, and women. Around nine, Peter announced that we had to sleep as we would ride tomorrow to the first water hole.

He lay down a sleeping bag and told me to slide into it and cover myself because it would become cooler and cooler. I slipped into the sleeping bag and tried to cover myself with the cover laying next to me. It was a leather blanket so heavy I could not lift it. I decided that I was warm enough and went to sleep. An hour later, I woke up freezing. Swallowing my pride, I called Peter and admitted I could not adequately cover myself. Peter laughed, made me promise that I would not be afraid to ask next time, and gently covered me. We all went back to sleep.

The next day we rode to the water hole. In the middle of the desert was an enormous hole filled with clear blue water. Peter said to undress and swim. It would refresh me; he added that for the next hour, he and John would go for a walk. And so I bathed in the coolest and most refreshing water I had ever felt.

Then it was my turn to go for a walk while they bathed. I walked toward a baobab tree. I hadn't seen one since Tanzania. The hole of its trunk was full of water. There were multicolored birds drinking from its trunk. I saw lizards at least twenty inches long, gliding on the sand and small rodents running around. The color of the sand was continually changing from a light pink to dark ochre. The desert was varied and incredibly beautiful, nothing like the desert outside of Cairo, where for miles you saw nothing but yellow sand.

For the next two days, we went from water hole to water hole, finally reaching our goal, the Aborigine village. The head or chief of the village was a woman, a tall giant of a woman with black hair and large black eyes. She wore a skirt and a wool sweater torn at the elbows. The village was formed of austere square concrete houses with a central communal building and a school near the edge of the settlement. The village looked and was very poor.

Peter explained that one of the reasons he wanted to build up this camel-trekking enterprise was to help the Aborigines of this particular and very special village.

"Why special?"

"They were the only ones willing to work with me. The only ones to promise to open up their village."

That night, dinner was served under the baobab tree. The women and children sat in a circle around a fire that an elder had built. A woman was roasting what looked liked very large corn kernels.

"Peter, what are these?"

"These are grubs, large silk worms that grow in the roots of trees around here. They are really delicious. Babies and young children are fed raw ones, and the adults eat them cooked over charcoal."

And picking one up with a metal fork, he handed it over to me. It did taste like roasted corn and was very good. I asked for more; the women laughed and seemed pleased that I liked their food. We ate Peter's bread with dark red berries, drank beer, and listened to an Aborigine man blowing on a long, wooden flute. It's a didgeri-doo, explained Peter, the oldest instrument on Earth.

The sound was in a low pitch, something like the soft moan of a bird. While he played, the women and children sang. Their song told the story of the desert, of hunting, and of animals. It was just beautiful and very sad.

We left the next morning. This time we took a short cut and took only a day and half to reach the camel ranch. Exhausted but pleased that I had survived, I flew to Sydney. I was going to be in Sydney for another three days, then on to Melbourne, then back to New York. The next two weeks went like a dream. I felt ener-gized by my trekking trip. I had thought a lot about what I wanted to do. I was going to write about my trip and then write about the Aborigine village and the courageous woman who ran it.

For the next few days, I explored Sydney, met with young chefs, visited markets, and drank a lot of beer. Then I traveled to Melbourne to meet with young Australian artists. I had a new idea every five minutes. I felt excited and eager to return home. During the camel trek, I had often thought of Jimmy. I realized then how much I loved him and how lonely I was without him. He was not only my husband and lover but also my best friend. I longed to see him. I felt that from now on we should share everything, work and play. On the fifteenth, Jimmy picked me up at the airport, and we drove home.

"I missed you. How was your trip? You look great."

"I missed you to, but I am tired. Give me a day, and I will tell you all about it. Such an exciting country!"

A week later, I started to write the trekking story. I kept in touch with the Aborigine village and Peter. His trekking venture was slowly picking up, and he hoped that soon he could hire more help.

Six months later, once again, I left on a trip: to Corsica for *European Travel*. I felt good and full of energy. On my return, I started a column "Ask Colette" for the *Daily News*. I loved to write this column. I would receive about twenty letters a week. Some were from older women who would ask me about recipes that they used to cook but had now forgotten how to prepare. Others were from younger women who wanted to reproduce recipes that their mothers or grandmothers had prepared for them and today wanted to cook them for their own children. There were letters from men feeling lonely who wanted to correspond with someone. They wrote that my responses were like me chatting with them in the kitchen. Once I even got a letter from a prisoner who read my column and wanted a recipe for a clam bake. He wrote that as soon as he was out, he would prepare one and invite me to share it with him. After publishing the recipe, I never got my invitation or heard from him.

I wrote this column for ten years until the spring of 2004.

⋙⋘

MUSSELS WITH GARLIC AND WHITE WINE

Place 4 quarts of fresh mussels in a colander and wash under running water. Brush the mussels with a stiff brush and remove the beards.

In a large saucepan melt 4 tablespoons of sweet butter. When the butter is hot, add 2 minced garlic cloves and sauté for 3 minutes, then add 4 tablespoons of chopped parsley and cook for 2 minutes. Then add the mussels and 1 cup of dry white wine.

Add ground pepper, cover, and cook over high heat for 6–8 minutes or until all the mussels have opened. Place the mussels in a deep bowl and cover with the cooking juice.

Serve right away with French or Italian baguette.

Serves 4.

SAUTÉED FIDDLEHEAD FERNS
WITH POMEGRANATE

Place 1 pound of fiddlehead ferns in a large bowl, and cover with cold water. Lightly rub them with your hands to remove any brown layer. Drain and pat dry.

Cut the pomegranate in half over a bowl to catch the juice and remove the ruby red seeds.

In a large skillet melt 2 tablespoons of sweet butter. Add the fiddleheads and cook over medium heat for about 4–6 minutes. Sprinkle with salt and pepper and add 2 tablespoons of dry tarragon. Mix well. Place the fiddleheads in a bowl, add 4 tablespoons pomegranate seeds, and toss.

Serve with roast pork or chicken.

Serves 4.

BRAISED CARDOON WITH CLEMENTINES

Remove the first layer of stalks from a medium-size cardoon. Cut each stalk into 1-inch pieces. In a large saucepan, bring 2 quarts of chicken broth with 1 tablespoon of lemon juice to a boil. Add the cardoon, bring to a boil, lower the heat to medium, and cook the cardoon for 15 minutes.

Drain and refresh under cold running water. Drain again. Remove any visible strings from the cardoon and peel.

In a saucepan melt 4 tablespoons of butter. When the butter is foamy add the cardoon, 1 tablespoon of lemon juice, salt and pepper to taste, and 1 tablespoon of dry sage. Lower the heat and cook for 30 minutes or until tender.

Meanwhile, cut the 4 clementines in half and remove any pits. In a large skillet melt ¾ cup of sugar with ¼ cup of water and cook for 5 minutes. Just before the sugar begins to color add the clementines, 4 at a time and cook for 5 minutes turning them once so that they are glazed all over. Transfer them with a slotted spoon onto a sheet of greased aluminum foil.

Place the cardoon on a serving platter, sprinkle it with chopped parsley and garnish the platter with the clementines.

Serves 4.

GREEN GRAPE TART

Make a pie dough. Butter a 9-inch pie pan and dust with flour. Line the pie pan with the dough and crimp the edges. Prick the dough with a fork and line with wax paper. Fill with raw rice. Bake in a 375° oven for 30 minutes. Remove from the oven and cool. Discard the rice and the paper.

In a food processor place 4 egg yolks and 2 egg whites, 4 tablespoons of flour, ½ cup of sugar, 1 cup of milk, ¼ cup of heavy cream and ½ cup of almonds.

Process for 1 minute. Pour the mixture in a saucepan and cook over medium heat, stirring all the while until the sauce thickens and coats a wooden spoon. Remove from the heat and cool.

Place 2 cups of sugar in a saucepan with ⅔ cup of water and cook over medium heat, stirring constantly until the sugar has completely dissolved and turns a golden color. Remove from heat.

Wash 1¾ pounds of grapes. Remove the grapes from their stems. Drain and pat dry. Pour the cream in the pie pan; place the grapes in concentric circles on top and brush with the melted sugar. Refrigerate until ready to serve.

Serves 6.

STEAMED FLOWERING KALE
WITH VEAL AND GINGER SAUCE

Preheat oven to 200°.

Cut 1 pound of thinly sliced veal in thin strips about ⅛ x 2 inches. Twist each strip and bring the ends together to form a circle. Attach with a toothpick. Dust the circles lightly with flour. In a skillet, heat ¼ cup of oil. When the oil is hot, add 3 chopped garlic cloves, sauté until golden, then add the veal circles and sauté quickly, turning just once until golden brown. Sprinkle with salt and pepper. Transfer the veal to a hot platter. Remove the outer leaves of a large flowering kale. Steam the kale for 10 minutes or until tender. Place the kale on a large platter. Sprinkle with salt. With kitchen shears, cut several leaves and arrange on individual plate likes the petals of a flower. Remove the toothpicks from the veal circles. Place in the center several veal circles. Sprinkle the dish with pink peppercorns and chopped cilantro. Drizzle with olive oil and serve.

MIZUMA TEA SANDWICHES

Trim the crust of 1 loaf of white bread, thinly sliced. Wash ½ of *mizuma* (Japanese salad grown in California) and pat dry with paper towel. Coarsely chop ¼ pound of smoked salmon. Place the salmon and 18-ounce package of cream cheese and mix well with a fork. Spread the cream cheese mixture on half the bread slices. Top with the *mizuma* leaves and cover with a slice of bread. Cut each sandwich diagonally and stack, pyramid fashion on a serving platter. Cover the sandwiches with a damp kitchen towel or seal with plastic wrap until ready to serve. The *mizuma* can be replaced with chopped watercress.

SPAGHETTI SQUASH WITH CRANBERRIES

Cut 1 medium-size spaghetti squash in two, lengthwise. Scoop out and discard the seeds. Place the squash in a large saucepan, add water to cover, cover the saucepan, and bring to a boil. Then lower the heat to medium. Cook until tender or about 20 minutes. Melt 2 tablespoons of butter in a saucepan. Add 1 heaping

tablespoon of finely chopped fresh ginger and 1 heaping tablespoon of finely chopped shallots. Sauté until the shallots are soft,
and then add 1 12-ounce package of fresh cranberries, 1 cup of
water, and 3 tablespoons of sugar. Bring the mixture to a boil,
season with salt and pepper, and cook, stirring occasionally until
the sauce is thick. Drain the spaghetti squash and remove the
flesh with a fork. Place the spaghetti squash in a large serving
bowl and top with the cranberry sauce. Serve with roast chicken.

With the cooks in China

8

The Silk Road

⋙⋘

In 1980, I met Peter Lee, a young Chinese restaurateur, through a friend, Clara B. Clara's job was to help Chinese immigrants adapt to New York life and assist them when they wanted to open businesses and maneuver through the city's intricate bureaucracies. Peter had come from Hong Kong a few years before and had saved enough money to open a Chinese restaurant. The restaurant opened to rave reviews, including mine in *New York* magazine, and Peter was on his way to becoming another immigrant success story. Very quickly, we became good friends. Together we explored all the new Chinese restaurants, and I became very knowledgeable in the different styles of Chinese Cuisine.

Meanwhile, in 1985, Jimmy was asked by the United Nations

to go to Bhutan. Every year, Asian countries who were members of the South East Asian Organization hosted, each in turn, a week long conference. Bhutan needed a conference center, and Jimmy was chosen as the designer for Bhutan's first conference center.

One day while Jimmy was in Bhutan, Peter came to me with a project. He wanted to make a film in China. It seemed that Chinese authorities, realizing the popularity of Chinese food in the United States, had decided to open a new cooking school outside of Beijing to teach young Chinese the art of Chinese Imperial Cuisine. To accomplish this, they had brought out of exile the aging Imperial chefs to teach the new generation who grew up during the Cultural Revolution how to cook. They believed a return to Imperial Chinese cooking traditions would bring tourists and dollars to the mainland. Peter believed I was the perfect person to make a film about this new cooking school. I liked food and was very familiar with Chinese cuisine, at least the Chinese cuisine of Chinatown.

Travel was very difficult in China in those years. Many places were not open to tourists and permission to enter China to make a film required great patience. I was daunted by all the obstacles, but Peter urged me to agree to go with him to China, and he explained that he would take care of me there. He had friends in high places, and many doors would be opened for me as long as I presented myself as a filmmaker interested in the cooking school.

I had always dreamed of going to China. I was also very interested in the Chinese Muslim population there. I had read that they were the largest minority in China and that during the Cultural Revolution, they had defied the government and kept their customs and dress. They also had received a food allowance from the government since Muslims did not eat pork, and lamb was more expensive. I wanted to see if there were remaining food traditions that recalled Arab influences. Going there and exploring the Silk Road had been one of my dreams. Peter agreed that once the film was made, we would explore Muslim towns.

However, I knew nothing about filmmaking and needed to add a professional to the team. I approached a few friends who introduced me to a young film director, Joseph G. Joseph had made several successful documentaries, but he knew nothing about food. He was, however, enthusiastic about going to China. When I expressed my doubts about doing a film on a cooking school, he said, "Don't worry I will take care of everything. We will need two cameramen. You will tell me what is important and unique, and I will take care of the rest. We will also need Peter to help us translate. Let's write a proposal and show it to the Public Broadcasting System, Channel 13."

PBS agreed to the project, made easy for them to approve because the Chinese government was funding the trip. I approached *The New York Times Magazine* and proposed a story on Arab food traditions among the Muslims in China, a story I would research by exploring the Silk Road. The editors felt that this was a fascinating food story. Suzanne Chen, my Chinese friend who had first introduced me to Chinatown, promised that her family would give me the names of people in China who could help me. They researched the names of restaurants, told me more about Islamic China, and what mosques in Guangzhou and Beijing were worth visiting.

We were ready to go; the only thing left was to obtain a visa. Once we had a commitment from PBS, Peter and I filed dozens of forms, and we were ready to leave. A week before we were scheduled to go, Peter arrived at our house and told me that a visa for him and me had come through, but that Joseph's and the cameramen's visas would come later. They would meet us in Beijing. He suggested that we first spend a week in Hong Kong. Joe was upset, but Peter was confident that their visas would come in time and that we would meet in Beijing in two weeks.

Hong Kong overwhelmed me: the noise; the crowds; the tall, modern buildings; but most of all the food. The Peking duck in Hong Kong was the best I had ever had with its crackling skin, its tiny pancakes made with rice flour and black sesame seeds, the duck meat tender and succulent. I tried drunken shrimps for the first time: Live shrimps are put in a bowl covered with rice wine, to get drunk before you eat them. I had never seen nor eaten so many different varieties of seafood, from razor clams to ten different types of shrimps, lobsters, crabs, and oysters. But what I liked best were the Chinese markets and street food. Ducks, chicken, barbequed birds, and sausages hung in open stands. Vegetables were piled high. Dozens of different kinds of Chinese cabbage from Chinese flowering cabbage to Chinese flat cabbage to bamboo mustard cabbage where the leaves, big and curled, were attached to a long, root-like stem. I saw barrels filled with four types of bean curd, from bean curd so light and soft that it was eaten with a spoon to firm bean curd for frying. I ate tiny barbequed birds on a skewer, just like how we used to eat them in Cairo in the fall. I tried tripe, rice noodles with shrimp and pork, broiled tofu, and many more delectable dishes such as agar-agar smoked ham salad, shark's fin with Chinese cabbage, lotus leaf rolls, and golden coin mushrooms.

Meanwhile, Peter was organizing our trip to mainland China. He introduced me to his "high placed" friends, whispering in my ear, "These are very important people. Like the Italian Mafia in New York. They're helping us to make the trip there easy."

"What about Joe and the crew?" I asked every day.

Peter's answer was always the same: "Don't worry; they'll meet us in Beijing."

A week later, with the help of Peter's "friends," we got two first-class seats on a train to Guangzhou. Peter was extremely excited to enter China again. He had not been home for close to fifteen years. He was carrying an attaché case that he kept near him at all the times. "Dollars," he whispered to me. "To open all doors in China."

We were met at the station in Guangzhou by a shabby looking man who spoke English well. Henry (all the people I met in China who dealt with foreigners had two names: one Chinese and one Western) was to be my translator. I called him my spy because he followed us everywhere. Henry smoked cheap cigarettes endlessly; and while we were driving around the town, he would point out garish new buildings with great pride. I learned that he was single. "Too expensive to get married, no apartment," he would tell me. For Henry, learning English was the door to a better life.

Since I was traveling with Peter, I was considered by the government to be, like Peter, an "overseas Chinese." We were housed not in American hotels, but in Chinese luxury hotels or guest houses where no one spoke English. Henry handed me a schedule for the next five days. I was expected to visit a school, a food-processing factory, a calligraphy museum, and other sites in which I had no interest. I told Henry that I wanted to visit the Muslim quarter and market, the mosque, and several restaurants that friends in New York had recommended to me.

The next few days were a nightmare. I was bored visiting factories and eating in hotels, and each time I asked Henry about restaurants I wanted to see or markets I wanted to go to, the answer was "They are closed; it is too far . . . it no longer exists." Peter was no help with Henry because he was always away organizing the trip to Beijing, Xi'an, and Harbin. This is when I decided to take things into my own hands.

Every night when Henry brought me back to the hotel after one of his boring trips, he would say, "Are you alright? Are you tired? Do you want to sleep late, or shall I pick you up at eight?" This time when Henry popped the usual questions, I said that I was very tired, that I wanted to sleep late, and that could he pick me up at eleven.

The next morning I got out of the hotel at six o'clock. Across from our hotel was a park. I walked over and saw men and women of all ages doing Tai Chi. The streets were jammed with bicycles pedaled by people going to work. I took a long walk, found a market, and saw vendors selling different types of noodles, vegetables, meat, and live poultry. There were also poor and forlorn old people selling their few possessions. By ten o'clock, I was famished. I found a sidewalk restaurant. The smell of the cooking food was intoxicating. Without hesitation, I sat down and had a bowl of soup filled with rice noodles, pork, and dried shrimps. Then I ate steamed white chicken stuffed with scallions and was given a dipping sauce made with grated ginger, scallions, and oil. The chicken was moist and tender and the sauce spicy: the best food I had had in a week. Suddenly I realized that I only had dollars in my purse. How was I going to pay for this great breakfast? With gestures to the cook, I tried to explain my lack of Chinese money and handed him a five-dollar bill. The cook laughed, pocketed the money, and offered me a dessert made with tapioca and melon. It was refreshing, not sweet, enchanting; alone worth the five dollars.

Suddenly I looked at my watch, it was 11:30 A.M. I was late, and I did not know exactly where I was. I saw a taxi passing by and stopped him. However, how do you tell a taxi driver where your hotel is in Chinese? The only name I knew was for foreigners. I remembered that the day before, at breakfast, I had put my chopstick cover in my pocket. If I were lucky, the name of the hotel would be there in Chinese. I showed it to the driver. He shook his head, motioned me to get in, and to my dismay, drove me to the Hilton. I was then nearly an hour late. Once at the Hilton, I explained to the manager that I was an overseas Chinese, showed him the name of the hotel on the chopstick cover. He called my hotel, and something serious must have transpired because suddenly the manager seemed worried and took me back to my taxi who accepted to drive me back after listening to the manager's angry voice.

Once in the hotel, I was faced with police, several stern men all dressed in black. *Secret police,* I thought; the hotel manager and Henry looked like guilty thieves. I was forcefully reminded that I could not leave the hotel without telling everyone where I was going. I looked at all of them and said very angrily, "I am not going to visit any more factories or schools. I came here to do a story for *The New York Times.* I have a list of places I want to visit, like restaurants where I want to eat, and if they do not want me to do it, I am returning to New York tomorrow!" A silence greeted my outburst. They all huddled together, then finally Henry came to me and said, "We will do what you want. I will take you to the mosque and to the restaurants that you want to visit, but you must promise not to disappear again." I was astonished by my success and made myself a promise that anytime they would refuse to do what I wanted, I would raise my voice and threaten to leave.

I then called Doctor Chan, a Chinese university professor, a friend of Suzanne's father. He agreed to show me around. During the next few days, we visited a tenth-century mosque, ate in Muslim restaurants, and visited markets and stores for foreigners. I now looked more favorably on Henry, so I bought him a carton of American cigarettes after he promised he would never again smoke in the car. A few days later, Peter, Henry, and I flew to Beijing.

Once in Beijing, Peter told me that the Chinese government had turned down Joe's and the camera crew's visas. They would not be coming. I was furious with Peter. I screamed at him for having misled me. His face became redder and redder. He tried to calm me down, to apologize, but I would not let him finish his sentences. I started to cry, still screaming, "What am I going to do? I had committed myself to making a film and now have no way of making it."

I realized then that Peter knew all along that Joe and the others would not come to China. "Colette, please don't worry; the film association is going to provide me with a crew; I will pay for everything." But I had never made a film and had no idea how to proceed. I was in a ridiculous situation, having come all the way from New York, ending up in a weird Chinese Hotel with a man who did not understand any of the problems I was facing.

There was just one thing to do: call Jimmy in Bhutan and ask for help. "Please. You're an artist; you will know what to film. Please help me." Peter, by now, afraid of me, promised to secure a visa for Jimmy. Jimmy arrived a few days later.

Together, we wrote a simple scenario and gave it to Peter to translate into Chinese for the film crew. I sat down with Peter, the cameramen, and the director and tried to explain what I wanted: footage of the school as we approach it, the students working, the chefs teaching, the finished dishes, etc.

The cooking school was located outside of Beijing, about an hour by car. It was housed in an old factory. The average age of the chefs and teachers was about seventy. They had been in exile for over a decade and were overjoyed to be back cooking and teaching. I attended cooking classes followed by the camera crew. I spent hours in the kitchen observing the chefs preparing elaborate dinners, teaching the young students how to carve radishes into flowers or Chinese pagodas. By observing them cooking, I learned about flavors, mixing ingredients, and vegetables: how to cut, slice, or chop; how to stir fry, and steam. To my surprise, I discovered that there were no ovens in the kitchens; just enormous steamers with very high temperatures. Large woks were placed over several circles of gas, and around them were pots filled with salt, pepper, spices, cornstarch, soy sauces, sesame oil, and water. All the ranges had spigots of boiling water. The heat was intense, the cooking incredibly fast. As there were no ovens in the kitchen, I wondered, *how did they bake those ducks that we had eaten the night before? Or those you see hanging in the windows of many food stores in Chinatown in New York?*

I learned that ducks were first immersed in boiling water then hung to dry in front of a fan overnight. Then they would be slowly lowered into boiling oil and cooked until crisp. Chickens and birds were also dried with a fan overnight before being cooked. Sometimes they were steamed, other times they were rubbed with spices before being cooked. I was told that there were four or five types of soy sauce, some with mushrooms, ranging from very dark and pungent to very light ones used for dipping sauce.

I saw the ancient chefs making incredibly long noodles in minutes, deboning ducks in a flash, and making dough for dim sum so thin that I thought it would fall apart when stuffed with meat or seafood. It never did. The camera men were always there, just behind me. Jimmy and I would tell them what to film; Peter would translate. At night we sat down to fabulous banquets. Then after dinner, the old chefs and I would sit down in the garden behind the school, and they would reminisce about their years in exile. Life had been very tough for them. They had been sent to far away villages, far from their families and the restaurants where for years they had toiled. They told me how they had learned to cook at a very early age and how famous their restaurants had been. It was all very sad, however, now they were proud to be back cooking again.

When after several days of filming and eating, we left to go back to Beijing, Peter told me that just before we left for the States, we would be given the cut and edited films.

Jimmy returned to Bhutan, and I continued my trip, first to Xi'an, a predominantly Muslim city. The market was similar to the one in Guangzhou, but it smelled like a Cairo market. The smell of cumin and coriander was in the air. There were piles of pita bread. But everything was different from Egypt. Pita, which are soft and round in the Middle East, were here round but dry and thick. They were used to mop up the sauce of lamb stew or were added to thicken lamb and vegetable soup. There was fried falafel as in Egypt, but here in China, you got small, round balls served with a spicy soy sauce. We went to a restaurant where I ate snake. A man brought us live snakes in a cage, and we were to choose, each of us, one that we liked. The snake meat tasted something like a sweet fish or chicken. They offered me the bile, a great honor I was told. If I drank it, I would stay young forever. I said yes. They added it to a glass of Matai, a very strong alcohol drink. My host smiled and was very pleased to see me enjoy the food.

The next day we ate in the largest restaurant I had ever seen. There must have been at least 100 tables that sat ten people each, like in Chinatown. The restaurant only served steamed dumplings, hundreds of varieties of them. All very small and of every possible shape: round ones, some triangular, or looking like buns; some were shaped into swans, others like jumping rabbits. They arrived steaming at the table in immense baskets and were usually served with three different sauces. One could eat 100 of them in the blink of an eye. I never had eaten anything so enchanting. We drank lots of tea and ended the meal with a chicken broth with some vegetables floating in it. Later Peter, Henry, and I flew to Harbin. I was still quite angry with Peter. I hadn't quite forgiven him for not being honest with me. But I was not only having a great time but also I was learning a lot.

In Harbin, we were met by Mongolian Chinese dressed in traditional costumes. We were housed in yurt huts, and ate with our hands, cross-legged on the floor with male members of the tribe. As in the Middle East, the women's faces were veiled, and they ate separately; young girls served us. We ate shish kebab, crisp cucumbers with mint, broiled lamb chops topped with goat yogurt, and steamed rice with chopped mint and yogurt. Desserts were pastries laden with honey and stuffed with nuts. At night, we sang songs and slept on the floor, covered with thick carpets.

A few days later, we flew back to Hong Kong. I constantly asked Peter where the tapes were. I was desperate to see them and frankly petrified. *How did we do, Jimmy and I? Would the videos be interesting? Why was no one willing to give them to me right away?*

"Don't worry," Peter kept on saying, "we will get them before you leave." The day of my return to New York, just before I left for the airport, Peter handed me six videotapes. He informed me that he was staying behind in Hong Kong for business.

On my return to New York, after a few days of rest, I had an appointment with PBS to review the tapes. I still had not seen them because they were professional tapes that did not fit in my small VCR. We all sat in a viewing room with Jay Iselin, the president of Channel 13, and several producers. I was anxiously waiting to see if we had something Channel 13 could show. From the first reel, I knew we had a disaster. The tapes were about me and not the school. They were also a sort of publicity film for China. The camera was following me; there were close-ups of my face, trying some food or talking to students. There were practically no images of the chefs, no pictures of students working in the kitchen, or for the banquets. No images of the food; nothing we could use. It was all about me!

I was upset and angry with Peter. I had wasted so much time and effort for nothing. I called David Low, a friend of Peter's that I had met before going to China. David explained that this was typical of Peter. He needed contacts in China and had used me as an excuse to enter China. It had all been a ruse.

At least I had had an exciting trip, learned a lot about China and Chinese food, made many friends, and hoped that one day I would go back. Jimmy had had fun, and I was proud of my article on Chinese Muslims and their food that was published in *The New York Times Magazine*.

I returned from expanding my horizons to take stock of my family and try once again to find my own place in the world.

Thomas graduated from Dartmouth and went on to Harvard to study architecture. There he fell in love with a fellow student who was studying law. Thomas and Rebecca waited until they both settled in New York before announcing that they were getting married.

After graduating from NYU, Marianne decided to make a film illustrating a poem of Edgar Allan Poe. The film was awarded a first prize for young directors in Paris, and she elected to stay there and make another film. Soon she announced that she was in love with a Frenchman. They got married in New York and settled here. It wasn't very long before she announced to Jimmy's and my delight that she was expecting our first grandchild. We were blissfully happy.

Jimmy had dissolved the firm of Conklin Rossant and had moved his office to the two top floors of our house. Now with Thomas and Cecile, we had three architects in the family. Jimmy decided his new firm would be called 3Rarchitects, just in case any of them would care to join him and work with him.

After finishing his studies, my nephew John had gone to work for *Business Week* and was living now in Rome, where he was their bureau chief. He had met a beautiful Calabrese woman who was working for the Italian Ministry of Foreign Affairs. Antonella and John were married by the mayor of Rome in a castle they had rented. Their wedding, which I catered, was the talk of the town.

And me? I was again looking for a steady job. One day I saw an ad in *The New York Times*. A large French bank was looking for a teacher to help their American vice presidents learn French. I was interviewed and landed the job. My work was child's play after all my years of teaching. I taught executives who needed to learn enough French to be able to understand their French counterparts and read memos that came from Paris. The salary was high, and I had ample time left to write articles.

One night I was invited to dinner by Karin Bakoum, an old friend who was half Egyptian like me. We always joked that we were the only two Egyptian witches in New York, as we claimed that we could read people's futures. During dinner, at my table sat the editor of *Saveur* magazine. Karin was telling stories about me, how I was a witch, like her; at least that's what *I* went around telling everybody. Laughingly, I told stories about growing up in Egypt, about fortune-tellers and my Egyptian grandmother's great food.

A few days later, I received a telephone call from *Saveur*. Would I be interested in writing a story about growing up in Egypt, what my life was like and especially what the food was like? I accepted eagerly and went to work. I taught in the morning at the bank, and in the evening, I wrote my story and tested the food. The story was published, and six months later, I was nominated for a James Beard award. I did not win, but the story, once expanded, became my first book of memoirs, *Apricots on the Nile*.

My mother was now seventy-five, still looking as beautiful and elegant as ever. She had stopped working at Lord & Taylor, but had registered for courses at the Art Studio school. She wanted to paint. She had painted when she was young, before she was married. All the students, young and old, loved her. If the weather was bad and she could not make her classes, they would call to see how she was or take her out for coffee or lunch. She was also making friends with the older women in the neighborhood whom she met at St. Anthony's parish at bingo games on Thursday nights and after mass on Sundays. They loved her as well; they talked to me about the way she dressed, her hat, and her lovely accent. They thought she was a great lady.

"You're so lucky to have her," they would say to me when I met them in the street. "Such a lovely lady."

I could not understand them. Who was this woman whom they liked so much? This woman who, when I was child, had abandoned me for five years, who never had seemed to care about me.

My children loved her.

The girls loved to hear her talk about the past when she was a rich young woman. She would show them photographs of her in a silk dress with pearls and a small dog on her lap. She would talk about her wedding. "It was the wedding of the year," she would tell them proudly. "The house was full of flowers; we had 400 guests. Your grandfather gave me a diamond broach on our wedding day. . . . We had our honeymoon in Venice."

"Grandmama, tell us, how did you meet him?"

"Well, my best friend at the lycee was an Egyptian girl. She was engaged to Mendès-France. You know he would become prime minister of France. I was invited to the wedding, and your grandfather was there. He was asked to choose which of the young bridesmaids he would like to walk down the aisle with. Guess who he picked? Me. We were married six months later."

My daughters enjoyed her stories and spent hours looking at her wedding pictures.

And I would be ignored!

I started to notice that my mother was losing weight. My mother, who had been on diets most of her adult life, suddenly now looked too thin. She tired more easily, and often when I came to visit, she would be either asleep in her chair near the window or sleeping in bed. It wasn't like her. I was still often angry with my mother because she kept on refusing to talk about the past, but I wanted her around me despite everything. I insisted that she see a doctor.

After a series of test, the news came in: She had advanced ovarian cancer and was dying. I wanted her to live. She was my last tie to my past. She had the memories; I didn't. She was going to die, and still I did not know why she deserted me years ago. I wanted to know what her life had been like those years when she had left me. What had happened to her to change her to the way she was now? I tried to talk to her, but to her last breath she refused. She had built a past that existed only in her mind. She kept on talking about my children, not me. The only personal thing she confided in me was what should happen when she died. She told me that she wanted her ashes to be thrown in the ocean so that they would float back to France. She died one night alone in the hospital. Strangely, I felt relieved. There were no more questions to ask.

For weeks, I procrastinated fulfilling her last wishes. Then one day, alone, I took her ashes and boarded the ferry to Staten Island. In the middle of the trip, I went on deck, looked around and threw the box in the water, hoping it would float toward France.

That night my friend Alan Buschbaum came to visit. Alan was my best friend. He was always there when I needed to talk about my problems. We talked about my mother. Like everyone else, Alan liked my mother. That night he made me laugh, recalling how the two of them would share recipes or talk about opera.

"Let's have dinner," Alan suggested cheerfully. "When I am sad, it is food I need, comfort food."

We ended up in the kitchen to cook dinner. Alan prepared his favorite dish, baked grits with cheese, and I sautéed chicken breast with lots of garlic and parsley. As the cooking aroma wafted through the kitchen, I felt better. As when I was a little girl, food, once again, was helping me cope with my pain.

However an unexpected loss would come and shatter our lives.

One night, Alan who had recently returned from a trip to Senegal with a friend, came for dinner and brought me a lovely present, a set of ivory bracelets. He looked tired, but then I assumed it was just jet lag. We chatted about his trip, my work, and the cooking school he had help create. He talked about Senegalese food, soups and stews he had loved and would cook for me in the following weeks. I did not see Alan for a few months. I kept on calling him, asking to come over, but he kept on getting the flu, or at least this is what he said he had. I asked him to come and live with us for a while so that I could take care of him. He refused. "I'll be fine. I have friends who help me, and I have to work. Let's have dinner together here as soon as my cold is over."

A few weeks later, when I called his office to invite him once again for dinner, I was told that he had pneumonia and was in the hospital. I went to see him, but when I got there, I was led to a special hospice-like part of the hospital. Alan was segregated with other patients who, like him, had pneumonia. Alan was lying in his bed, pale, his eyes closed, looking so sick. I wanted to cry.

I heard him say in a very low voice, "Water, I'm thirsty." I saw no glass, only long, very large Q-tips. I went out and ask the nurse what to do.

"With AIDS patients, you take the Q-tips, soak them in water, and wet his lips. Don't touch anything; don't touch him and wash your hands."

I was aware of the disease that had been spreading, but AIDS hadn't been made real for me until that day. This is how I learned that Alan had AIDS. It explained his flu symptoms and his tiredness. I was horrified and sad.

I tiptoed back to his room, did what the nurse had told me to do, and as I was wetting his lips he opened his eyes, looked at me and murmured, "Go, go, leave me." After a few minutes, I did.

I realized, thinking of the past, that Alan had never wanted me to know he was gay. Despite our lasting friendship, he did not think I would approve. He was so wrong. I had known for years and was completely comfortable with him. We flirted, but I knew it was all a game. I trusted him; he was my best friend. I felt sad and also betrayed that he had not trusted me in return.

I called the hospital every day to see how he was, but he never wanted to speak to me. Once he was back home and feeling better, he came by to see me. Once again we cooked together, talked together, but never did he mention my visit to the hospital, and I did not know what I was supposed to say or do.

A few months later, Alan was back at the hospice. This time both Jimmy and I came right away. When Jimmy left the room, I sat down near him and told him I knew he was gay, that it made no difference to me, that I was his friend, and that he had to trust me. "I am sorry, Colette; you must forgive me. This is very hard. I hate what this disease is doing to me. I don't want to die . . ."

I was broken hearted to see him like this. We had been so close to him. We knew his mother and his sister. Years ago, when I wanted to write about Savannah, he had helped me. We stayed with his family. I felt he was like my brother. I was loosing my best friend to this horrible disease that would take so many lives in the years that followed.

A few days later, Alan died. There was a memorial for him. Half of Soho came, also celebrities for whom he had designed apartments or lofts. Both Marianne and Juliette wrote and read poems. Of all our children, Marianne was the most affected. They had been close, and when she had a problem with a relationship, instead of talking with us, she went to him for advice. He then would help me to understand what was happening to Marianne. Alan's death was a great loss for the whole family.

Once again we redoubled our efforts to protect our children from the outside world. We became more involved in their lives, trying to help them avoid being too hurt when joining the adult world. We didn't always succeed.

Looking back, I realized that I was then too involved in their lives and often interfered by trying to solve their problems when I should have let go of my children. Despite that, like many other couples in these troubled times, we sometimes failed but still managed to remain a close knit family.

Juliette, always the most adventurous, had gone to Istanbul,

Turkey to teach. While teaching in Istanbul, Juliette, very entrepre-
neurial, managed to get Jimmy an exciting new architectural job:
the design of a new gymnasium for her school. While the gymnasium was being built, we went several times to Turkey to visit.

On her day off, Juliette and I explored the bazaar, ate in a
small restaurant, and visited markets. My Egyptian grandmother
was born in Istanbul, and I felt very at home there. However,
Juliette soon grew bored with teaching English to wealthy Turkish girls, and later college students, and decided to become a
journalist. It was during the time of the first Gulf War. Because
she was fluent in Turkish, she was hired by *Business Week*. Her first
big break came when she covered the Gulf War on the Turkish-
Iraqi border. She wrote from Cizre about the plight of the Kurds
who were crossing the border from Iraq into Turkey. When the
war was over, she reported on the Kurdish refugee camps where
hundreds were dying. She also had a by-line for *The New York Post*. I
learned about her exploits by reading the paper. When the war
was over, Juliette continued to write for *Business Week*. She covered the war in Azerbaijan, one of the former Soviet Republics in
the Caucasus. She sent dispatches about a fierce battle between
Armenians and Azerbaijanis as witnessed from a helicopter also
under fire. We learned all of this through her articles, living in
fear that something terrible might happen to her.

Later, she wrote about the effect of the war on the Turkish econ-
omy, and at the same time, she was also falling in and out of love.
First she fell deeply in love with a Turkish teacher, but this did not
work. Later she fell in love with a French journalist who whisked
her away to Moscow. This did not turn out either, but Juliette, still
the great adventurer, learned Russian and was a witness of the
Russian uprising in Moscow and the burning of the Russian "White
House." From Russia, she took many trips to Central Asia, to Turk-
menistan, Kazakhstan, and Uzbekistan. To our great relief, she

came back to New York in one piece and started to work for *Forbes*. She had fallen in love with a bright American who was working in Saudi Arabia. David spoke Arabic and loved the Middle East. Marriage was in the air, and we felt very happy for her.

But it was Cecile who we worried about the most. She had taken years deciding what she wanted to do and finally decided to follow in Jimmy's footsteps and study architecture. After graduating from Princeton as an architect, Cecile had a problem finding work. New York was in a recession and work for young architects was sparse. She worked for Jimmy's office for a few months then for Arakawa, our artist friend. When Arata Isozaki, a Japanese architect and our friend, came to New York, he told Arakawa he needed young architects for his office in Tokyo. Arakawa suggested he hire Cecile. Arata said he would be eager to take on Cecile, and so for a while, Cecile worked at Arata's New York office and then left for Tokyo to join the main office.

Much later, Jimmy was offered a spring show of his drawings in a prestigious gallery in Tokyo. We flew to Tokyo for the opening, and after a week in Tokyo, we spent time with Cecile. I was sad to leave Cecile alone again in Japan, but very soon letters and e-mail arrived full of good news. Cecile loved Japan, was learning the language very quickly, and was having a very creative time. By the fall, she had met a young Japanese architect and was deeply in love. At the next Christmas, they both arrived in New York. Ghen was a handsome and gracious man who loved music and art. He seemed to be a very talented architect, and most of all, he loved Cecile. We were delighted having them with us. When they were about to leave, being an interfering mother, I asked Ghen if he was going to marry Cecile: His answer was "I ask her every day, but she says she is happy as we are."

A month later Cecile called, "We are getting married. But the wedding has to be in Japan because Ghen's grandfather is too old to come to New York, and Ghen wants him to be present. You don't have to do anything. We are designing the wedding."

Cecile had been our most restless child, and we were ecstatic that she had finally found someone who shared her ideas about life. Although disappointed that the wedding would not take place in New York and that once married they would continue to live in Japan, I already was planning trips back and forth in my mind.

A few weeks before the wedding, we were awakened at two in the morning by a telephone call from Cecile. Ghen had died suddenly in her arms. The cause was a brain aneurysm. We learned to our horror that she had tried to get help from neighbors, but doors were slammed in her face, and when the ambulance had finally arrived, it was too late.

The next morning I flew to Japan to be with her. What do you say to your child when her world collapses? When you look at her and see how deep the hurt is? You say nothing; you are simply there. You hold her hands, you let her cry, and you stay by her side. The funeral was long and arduous. I stayed a week longer than I intended. I hated leaving her alone in the tiny apartment she had shared with Ghen. I wanted her back with us, but she adamantly refused. She was staying in Japan.

Months went by. Every time I called I could hear the tears in her voice. I had to help her get out of Japan. Jimmy and I decided that we had to talk to Arata Isozaki. I knew in my heart that I should not interfere, but I could not stand her pain and thought, right or wrong, that once out of Japan where everything reminded her of Ghen, she might feel better. Arata was an internationally renowned architect who had projects around the world. We begged him to send Cecile somewhere, anywhere out of Japan.

A few months later, Cecile announced that Arata Isozaki was sending her to Berlin to help with the building of a large project. Cecile had been in Berlin two years when she announced near

Christmas that she was visiting us with a new wonderful friend. Christian, her future husband, came into our lives, and we hoped that Cecile had recovered from Ghen's death and would be able to rebuild her life.

Meanwhile, Matthew, our first grandchild, was born.

Two years later, Marianne announced she was pregnant again; Thomas and Rebecca were married; and Juliette was seriously in love with David. They got married in Jordan, but they were moving back to New York.

A year later Julien, Marianne's second little boy, was born. The family was growing.

As time went by, the family changed and grew even more. Two years after Julien was born, Marianne divorced and was living in Brooklyn with her two little boys. She had become very involved in education. She was now taking a degree in education at the New School University as she had decided to follow her dream of creating new, radical, smaller schools. She had met a young man, Edi, who shared her dreams. Together, once she graduated, they would move to Santa Barbara, California, to try and establish their dream school.

Thomas was designing very exciting projects at a leading New York firm while being totally absorbed by his lovely baby son, Luca.

Cecile had married Christian. She now lived in Berlin. She was still working as an architect but had also begun to write and was finishing a book of short stories. Her daughter, Celine, was saying her first words of English. Cecile was also expecting her second child.

Meanwhile, our house on Sullivan Street felt different. Our children had flown the coop, and the house seemed deserted, too vast for both of us. Jimmy decided to remodel the house.

"Let's build an apartment downstairs. It will bring us much

needed income." I protested. I loved my house, my garden. I would lose my kitchen and dining room. But Jimmy promised to build me a new kitchen, better than the one I had downstairs, and a dining room with a copper dome.

"A *tempieto*," he called it. "A small temple of food, just for you."

Jimmy was very excited about this project. This was the first time that he was designing and building something new for us. I was often upset as for a month we camped in a house that was under construction, going back to our beginnings, often cooking in the fireplace while the new kitchen was being built. My lovely garden was trampled by the construction workers. I was getting very impatient, but then one day the project was finished and the downstairs apartment was rented. The *tempieto* was lovely, full of light with a great view of my lovely garden. Once again, I started to cook, inspired by my *tempieto*. We threw an enormous house-warming party, and all of New York seemed to be there. Friends, children, and grandchildren's laughter filled the house, a flowering hibiscus grew in the kitchen balcony, and my roses bloomed once again.

It is Christmas Eve, and all our children are gathered in our Soho town house. Two days ago, Thomas and I went to buy a Christmas tree. Tonight we will decorate it with Christmas ornaments that we have accumulated over the years. My favorite ones are the ones we bought when our children were very young on our trip to Guatemala. Our friend, Philip Herrera, had suggested the trip and had given us the use of his house on Lake Atitlán. All around the lake were small villages where we bought these ornaments from a local artist. They are made of straw but look like gold in the glow of the tiny Christmas lights. There are other charming ornaments that our friends have brought us. For the past twenty years, we have given a party, inviting our friends to be with our children and grandchildren. Every guest had to bring something for the tree. I usually asked that they make it, but they seldom did. Around midnight we serve dinner, I call it a Reveillon, like the French. I serve a four-meat pâté, *boudin blanc*, a veal sausage served with good mustard, lentils with lots of garlic, salad, cheese, tangerines, and a *bûche de Noël* that Jerome, the patissier from Once Upon A Tart down the street makes every year.

After midnight, when all the guests have gone, we bring the presents down from hiding places upstairs. Jimmy and Marianne usually have made the best packages. One year, the year that the astronauts went to the moon, Jimmy transformed all the gifts into an enormous space ship. Another year he and Thomas built the city of Bethlehem, with palm trees decorated with little lights behind the village.

I am always in charge of the stockings. This is what I like best. I roam the city choosing small, amusing, unusual, and often useless presents to fill the stockings. I hang them on the mantle piece, one for each member of the family, now seventeen. They are the first things we open in the morning before we have breakfast. The screams of delight of my grandchildren still resonate in my mind. Jimmy prepares breakfast. He is famous for his waffles. Since we've been married, now fifty years, Jimmy has always cooked breakfast on Christmas morning.

Christmas dinner is late at night. We all cook together. Marianne usually makes a soup. She makes a wonderful, pungent carrot and ginger soup. Thomas and I roast a goose, and I stuff the neck. This is a very old recipe that my French grandmother always made for Christmas. Juliette takes care of dessert, and Cecile, who half the time is vegetarian, cooks the vegetables. On this day, it is the only time where no one argues. Food in our family seems to still be the catalyst for bringing us together. We all sit, sixteen of us around a long table in the living room. It is the only time we eat there. As I look around the table, I remember that as a child I had never experienced this pleasure. Perhaps I have succeeded in my quest to create a real family, something I never had.

Two years later, Oliver, Thomas's second son, is born.

➤◄

CARROT SOUP

Peel, scrape, and cut in 1-inch pieces, 6 carrots. Place the carrots in a saucepan and cover with water and ½ teaspoon of salt. Bring to a boil, lower the heat, and cook for 15 minutes or until the carrots are done. Drain the carrots, reserving the liquid. Place the carrots in a food processor with 1 medium onion; a 2-inch piece of ginger, peeled and cut; 1 tablespoon of dried thyme, and 2 garlic cloves. Add 1 cup of the carrot water and puree. In a saucepan, bring to a boil 5 cups of chicken bouillon. Add the carrot puree and mix well. Correct the seasoning with salt and freshly ground pepper. Heat the soup, then pour it in 6 individual bowls. Top with 1 tablespoon of crème fraîche and garnish with 1 mint leaf.

Serves 6.

STUFFED GOOSE NECK

Preheat oven at 350°.

When preparing to roast a goose, first cut the neck skin of a 10-pound goose. Lay it flat and remove the veins and the fat inside the skin. Fold the skin in two. Start sewing it, using heavy thread in a darning needle, starting from the narrow end; leave the wider end open to stuff. In a bowl mix together 2 cups of pork sausages with 2 garlic cloves, 1 tablespoon of sage, 1 tablespoon of thyme, and 1 egg. Mix well. In a skillet, heat 2 tablespoons of butter. Add 2 shallots, chopped; the goose liver, cubed, and 2 or 3 chicken livers also cubed. Sprinkle with salt and pepper. Sautée for 5 minutes. Then pour over the livers 2 tablespoons of brandy and ignite. When the flame dies down, add the livers to the pork mixture and mix well. Stuff the neck and sew the last opening. Place the stuffed neck along side the goose. When the goose is cooked, remove the neck, let it cool, refrigerate, and serve as an appetizer, thinly sliced.

If you have too much stuffing, roll it like sausage, wrap it in foil paper, and bake it alongside of the goose.

ANNE'S BRISKET OF BEEF

Have the butcher trim most of the fat of a 5-pound beef brisket. Peel 6 garlic cloves and insert into the meat slivers of garlic. Place the meat in a large baking pan. Sprinkle with coarse salt and freshly ground pepper and 2 tablespoons of dried marjoram and thyme. Pour 2 tablespoons of dark soy mixed with 2 tablespoons of olive oil on the meat. Peel and thinly slice 2 medium onions. Spread the slices on top of the meat. Then add 3 cups of beef consommé to the pan. Cover the roasting pan with foil paper and bake in a 350° oven for 3 hours, adding more consommé if necessary. Remove the meat from the pan and thinly slice. Serve with the pan juices.

Serves 4.

KREPLACH

These kreplach are made with leftover brisket.

In a bowl, mix together 2 cups of flour with ½ teaspoon of salt, freshly ground pepper, and 3 tablespoons of oil. Mix well. In another bowl, beat 2 egg yolks with ½ cup of water. Add the egg mixture to the flour along with 1½ teaspoon of baking powder. Knead until you have a smooth dough. Roll the dough on a floured board as thin as you can.

Cut squares 3-inches on the side.

Cut the leftover meat in small cubes. You need about 2 cups of ground meat. Add some pan juices enough to moisten the meat. Then add 1 onion finely chopped and mix well. Correct the seasoning adding salt and pepper if necessary.

Place 1 teaspoon of the ground meat in the center of the square. Moisten the edges with water and fold the dough to form a triangle; press the dough down to seal the meat. Repeat this step until all the meat has been used.

In a saucepan bring 3 quarts of water to a boil. Add the kreplach and bring to a boil, lower the heat to medium. Cook until the kreplach rise to the top. Remove with a slotted spoon and add to a strong chicken soup.

Serves 4.

JULIETTE'S CHOCOLATE TRUFFLES

In a food processor place 2 tablespoons of unsweetened cocoa, 2 tablespoons of brandy, ¼ cup of walnuts, 4 tablespoons of butter, cut in small pieces, 2 cups of confectioner's sugar, 2 tablespoons of corn syrup, 1 tablespoon of heavy cream, and a pinch of salt. Process all the ingredients until the mixture is a thick paste. Remove to a bowl. Wet lightly your hands and roll the cocoa mixture between the palms of your hands into small balls about 1-inch in diameter.

Place ¼ cup of nuts (almonds, pecans, or hazelnuts) in a food processor and process until chopped fine. Transfer the chopped nuts into a bowl. In another bowl place ½ cup of cocoa. Roll the balls first in the chopped nuts then in the cocoa. Place the truffles in a sealed container and refrigerate for 24 hours.

Makes about 30 truffles.

Acknowledgments

The past few years, many people have helped me go through difficult times. First, I want to thank the Bogliasco Foundation, which offered me a haven of peace and quiet to write this book; my friend Rosemary Ahern for her editorial help and suggestions; my very good friend and agent Gloria Loomis for believing in me; Peter Borland, my editor at Atria who has beautifully edited this book; and finally my husband, Jimmy, without whom this book would never have been written.